Intelligence Builders for Every Student

44 Exercises to Expand MI in Your Classroom

David Lazear

Zephyr
Press ®

REACHING THEIR HIGHEST POTENTIAL

Tucson, Arizona

Intelligence Builders for Every Student
44 Exercises to Expand MI in Your Classroom

Grades 4–8

©1998 by Zephyr Press
Printed in the United States of America

ISBN 1-56976-069-1

Editor: Stacey Shropshire
Cover design: Daniel Miedaner
Illustrations: Stirling Crebbs
Design and production: Daniel Miedaner
Typesetting: Daniel Miedaner

Zephyr Press
P.O. Box 66006
Tucson, AZ 85728-6006
http://www.zephyrpress.com

Contents

How to Use This Book

The activities in this book are adapted from the series Step Beyond Your Limits. They are intended for students to do on their own. You may copy those that are appropriate for individual students, you may guide your students through developing individual intelligences, or you may guide them through an entire course in developing multiple intelligences. Whatever your MI needs, you can use this book to meet them.

Bodily-Kinesthetic Intelligence

Walking to Expand Your Awareness

*I Get Around!
Do You?*

> *Tailor the practices and exercises in this section to your walking patterns. If anything I suggest doesn't seem natural to you, change it. Give yourself time to get in touch with the various new walks before you try to integrate them into your daily walking.*

Walking Here and Walking There

Getting Started

Begin with the first exercise to get a feel for the power of walking and to intensify your awareness of how you already use walking. Use the second exercise to experiment and to plan walks that will help you deal with various issues and challenges you are currently facing in your life.

Basic Process

Exercise 1 of this practice starts with developing an awareness of the different kinds of walks that are already part of your life. Exercise 2 works with creating new styles of walking to help you deal with a variety of situations.

Exercise 1: Awareness of Everyday Walking

1. For a day, keep a record of every time you walk, anywhere, using a chart with the headings *Time* (When did I walk?), *Goal* (Where did I walk and why?), *Mood* (What was I feeling?), and *Style* (Describe how I was walking.).

2. At the end of the day, spend a few minutes reflecting on the chart. Ask yourself the following questions: What is the first thing I notice? What immediately grabs my attention? What patterns (if any) do I see? What do I find surprising? What do I see that is intriguing? What is bothersome or irritating?

3. Look at each row of the chart in turn, create a name for that type of walk and write the name in the margin, for example, the "thinking things over walk," or the "dealing with stress walk."

Exercise 2: Intentional Walking Experiment

1. Based on what you have learned about your normal walking patterns, create a walking plan for tomorrow, for example, "Tomorrow when I need to solve a problem, I'll go for a short 'thinking things over' walk."

2. At the end of the day, spend a few moments reflecting on how these intentional walks helped you deal with the day more effectively.

New Styles of Walking*

Getting Started

You will need time alone in a space where you will not be disturbed and where you have lots of room for walking (for example, a park, a gymnasium, or a field). You may want to treat each of the suggested walks below as a separate exercise (each will take about thirty minutes) or you may want to set aside two hours to try them all at once.

Basic Process

This practice asks you to experiment with walking to shift your awareness and mood. It involves the conscious use of walking and reflection. It will take you through four experimental walking exercises.

Exercise 1: Stability and Groundedness

We often talk about people who "really have their acts together." They are generally very practical, logical, rational individuals who know where they are going and how they are going to get there. We often say they "really have their feet on the ground."

1. Begin walking in a way that embodies the sense of being grounded, knowing exactly where you are headed and what you are about. Think about the earth beneath you and about planting your feet firmly on it. As you walk place your feet with certainty. Walk with purpose and intention, absolutely clear of your direction and goal. Walk as if there were a strong hand behind you, pushing you forward and supporting you. Walk as if nothing could stop you.

2. Stop and think of times or situations in your life when you need this kind of stability, purpose, and clear direction. Close your eyes and imagine that you are in one of these situations right now.

*Adapted from Lazear, David. 1991. *Seven Ways of Knowing: Teaching for Multiple Intelligences* (Palatine, Ill.: Skylight).

3. Start walking as before, but pretend that you are walking into this imagined situation. See yourself as a person with strong determination.

4. Stop and spend a few moments reflecting on how you can continue to practice this walk and use it to amplify your sense of stability.

Exercise 2: Openness and Flexibility

We all know people who seem to be deeply tuned in to other people and their needs. They are generally very sensitive people. They tend to be very flexible, adept at seeing things from a variety of perspectives, and good at the art of compromise when dealing with others.

1. Begin walking in a way that embodies this sense of flexibility, openness, and sensitivity. Think about the qualities of water, the way it flows and can change shape to fit almost any situation. Walk with great sensitivity and gentleness. Walk as though you were walking barefoot in soft grass. Walk as if you are totally one with the environment around you.

2. Stop and think of times or situations in your life when you need this kind of flexibility, openness, and sensitivity. Close your eyes and imagine that you are in one of these situations.

3. Start walking as before, but pretend that you are walking into this imagined situation. Walk into this situation as a person filled with compassion, flexibility, and sensitivity.

4. Stop and spend a few moments reflecting on how you can continue to practice this walk and use it to amplify your sensitivity to others.

Exercise 3: Confidence and Motivation

Some people seem to have a boundless supply of energy, as if a fire were raging within them. They seem to be filled with confidence and passion regardless of what they are doing.

1. Begin walking in a way that embodies this sense of confidence and passion. Your goals are clear and you are set steadfastly on getting there. Think about the qualities of fire, the way it moves very quickly, the way it consumes anything in its path, and the way, once it starts burning, it is hard to stop or contain. Walk while imagining the sun is burning in your abdomen; let its energy drive your walking. Walk with a clear vision of where you are going, like a sunbeam or a ray of bright light. Walk with a clear goal in mind. Walk as if you have no fear of anything.

2. Stop and think of situations in your life when you need this kind of confidence, passion, and energy. Close your eyes and imagine that you are in one of these situations right now.

3. Start walking as before, but pretend that you are walking into this imagined situation. Walk into this situation as a person filled with courage and intention.

4. Stop and spend a few moments reflecting on how you can continue to practice this walk and use it to amplify your sense of confidence and motivation.

Exercise 4: Inner Vision and Intuition

We sometimes meet people who have a profound sense of life's meaning. They are often perceived as deep thinkers. They are filled with a great deal of compassion and sensitivity.

1. Begin walking in a way that embodies a sense of wonder and awe, trying to feel a sense of vastness and a sense of oneness with all that is around you. This walk may feel more as though you were floating or flying than walking! Walk wherever your feelings lead you; don't analyze why you are walking there—just walk. Walk following your intuitions; this walk is almost like being transported. Walk trying to sense yourself expanding in all directions. Walk as if you were in a sacred place; imagine that every step has profound meaning.

2. Stop and think of times or situations in your life when you need this kind of cosmic perspective. Close your eyes and imagine that you are in one of these situations right now.

3. Start walking as before, but pretend that you are walking into this imagined situation. Walk into this situation as a person filled with inspiration and insight.

4. Stop and spend a few moments reflecting on how you can continue to practice this walk and use it to amplify your sense of the meaningfulness of your daily life and its connection with the larger patterns of the universe.

Multitracking Practices

How Many Things Can You Do at Once?

> *As you work with the exercises in this section, don't get cross with yourself if you can't do the full routine. Work slowly, adding one thing at a time until you feel you've got it. If you lose the ability to do one of the activities, return to a lower level.*

Multitracking

Getting Started

You will probably want to do the first exercise alone, for you will be performing a series of rather strange body movements. The second exercise will ask you to extend your multitracking capacities into your everyday life, and you can perform them when you are in ordinary situations with other people.

Basic Process

The exercises in this section build on one another; perform them in sequence. Exercise 1 asks you to experiment with increasingly complex routines. The intent of the second exercise is to help you weave connections in your brain.

Exercise 1: Programming the Body for Complexity*

1. Begin by slowly jogging in place. Begin moving your head from left to right. Then swing your your arms from left to right. Move your tongue inside your mouth from left to right. Stop and rest.

2. Begin jogging in place again, moving your head from left to right as before. Then swing your arms, but this time move them opposite the direction in which your head is moving. Next move your eyeballs up and down. Finally, move your tongue in tandem with your arm movements. Stop and rest.

3. Repeat the sequence of activities from 2, but this time do everything opposite; that is, jog in place while moving your head from right to left, swinging your arms from left to right, moving your eyeballs first down then up, and moving your tongue from right to left. Stop and rest.

4. Rrepeat the sequence from 2. Once you have everything going, add snapping your fingers, singing "Are You Sleeping, Brother John," mentally saying the "Pledge of Allegiance," and noting any smells in the environment. Stop and rest.

Exercise 2: Amplifying Multitracking in Everyday Living

1. Make a list of at least three times during your normal day when you are already engaged in simple, unconscious multitracking activities, for example, talking on the phone while you work on your computer; or walking, eating a candy bar, and talking to someone else.

2. For each situation, brainstorm two or three activities you could add to these routines that would increase their complexity, for example, while doing homework and watching TV, make a "to do" list for the next day and talk to your friend.

3. Make a second list of times during the day when you are only monotracking. Then brainstorm how you could turn these into occasions for multitracking. Following is a suggestion: **While eating your lunch,** pay full attention to the activity of eating, read a magazine, make a list of things you must accomplish in the afternoon, and listen to some music, subtly moving to its beat or rhythm.

4. Reflect on what happened as you practiced multitracking in your everyday life: What really stands out in my mind? What happened? What do I remember? What was especially interesting about this multitracking? What surprised me? What discoveries did I make? Some of the benefits of multitracking that I can see in my own life are . . . ? Where else do I want to practice multitracking? Where do I **need** to improve my multitracking capacities?

---

*Adapted from Lazear, David. 1991. *Seven Ways of Knowing: Teaching for Multiple intelligences* (Palatine, Ill.: Skylight).

Communicating with the Body

Actions Speak Louder Than Words

> *Although you can complete the exercises in this section in two days, feel free to alter this time frame. It is more important to gather accurate body language information than to complete your observations within a given period of time. In the second exercise (observing yourself) you may need to use a gimmick such as pretending you are watching yourself on TV or looking down from outer space—whatever works for you.*

Communicating with the Body

Getting Started

Choose two consecutive days, one for each exercise of this practice.

Basic Process

This practice asks you to experiment with consciously developing your capacities for using your body as a vehicle for enhancing, amplifying, and deepening communication with others.

Exercise 1: Awareness of Others' Body Language (simple)

1. Choose a typical day of your week. Use the chart on page 7 to help you become aware of others' body language. You are watching how various people use their bodies and for what purpose.

2. Reflect on your observations recorded on the chart: What immediately grabs my attention? Where do I see repeating patterns of gestures, postures, and physical movements? What surprises do I see? What is amusing? What is disturbing? What other feelings am I experiencing?

3. Try to classify the **different kinds** of body language you have observed, for example, actions that communicate empathy and movements that demonstrate boredom, tiredness, or stress. On a blank page see if you can categorize *all* of the observed gestures, postures, and other physical movements.

Situation	Gestures observed and purpose	Body postures observed and purpose	Other physical movements and purpose
Morning with the family:			
At school *(first observation):* Choose a typical situation.			
At school *(second observation):* Choose another typical situation.			
At school *(third observation):* Choose another typical situation.			
The family in the evening: Observe a normal, evening situation.			

4. Spend a few minutes reflecting on this exercise: What discoveries have I made? What have I learned from this exercise? What new insights have I gained?

Exercise 2: Awareness of My Own Body Language (complex)

1. Using a blank chart, repeat the body language observation process, this time focusing on yourself and your use of your body. **Note:** As much as possible try to be simply an outside observer. Don't alter your normal behavior. Simply record what you notice.

2. Reflect on the chart. Classify your own body movements.

3. Spend some time reflecting on and evaluating the effectiveness of your body language.

   ◆ What do I notice about my body language?

   ◆ What patterns of personal body language do I notice?

   ◆ What do I notice that surprises me? What does not surprise me?

   ◆ What do I see that amuses me? Disturbs me? Confuses me?

   ◆ Where does my body language adequately express what I am intending to communicate?

   ◆ Where does my body language fail to say what I mean?

4. Finally, complete the following sentences to create a strategic body language plan that is more in line with what you want to communicate. New body language strategies I want to try are . . . Alterations I want to make in my current body language strategies include . . . Existing body language patterns that I need to reinforce are . . .

Psychophysical Recovery of the Self Practices

I Act! Therefore, I Am!

Research has shown that many of the solutions to the challenges we face in our everyday lives are latent in our bodies. The following practice builds your capacities to tap your innate body wisdom.

Unblocking Future Goals*

Getting Started

You will need a relatively open space (a backyard, an open field, a gymnasium). You will probably want to work alone or with a friend. Make sure you will not be interrupted. Choose a piece of energizing instrumental music to use in the exercise.

*Adapted from Lazear, David. 1991. *Seven Ways of Knowing: Teaching for Multiple Intelligences* (Palatine, Ill.: Skylight).

Basic Process

The practice starts by asking you to think about your immediate future and your goals as well as the obstacles you may be facing. You will then go through a psychophysical process of dealing with those obstacles. The practice ends with time to revisit the original goals and reflect on what happened to them during the course of the practice.

Exercise 1: Analyzing Future Goals

Using a chart with the three headings *Goals, Obstacles,* and *Metaphors,* analyze several of your immediate goals for the future.

- In the "Goals" column, list three to five concrete goals that you have for the next year.
- In the "Obstacles" column, list obstacles that are making it difficult to achieve your goals, for example, attitudes, other people, policies, or values.
- In the "Metaphors" column, list metaphors that reflect the nature of the obstacles; for example, you may feel that one obstacle is a spider web that must be untangled; another might be a steep mountain that must be climbed.

Exercise 2: Psychophysical Exploration of Goals

Select at least three goals to work on in this exercise. Choose an energizing piece of instrumental music to play.

- Reflect on the obstacles related to the first goal. Think about the metaphors you have chosen.
- Start the music. Close your eyes and take several deep breaths. Get a mental picture of the metaphor.
- Move around the space, getting a feel for the music. As soon as you are ready, begin performing actions that are in line with the metaphor; for example, if the metaphor is a mountain that must be scaled, pretend you are scaling a mountain, experiencing in your body what it would be like to scale a mountain.
- While you are performing these symbolic activities, reflect on the specific obstacles. Focus on the specific obstacle and try to mentally and physically feel yourself dealing with it in and through the movements.
- When you feel you have successfully dealt with the obstacle, move on to another block for this goal, or start working on the second goal you chose.

Exercise 3: Reflecting on the Process

Turn off the music and sit down. Close your eyes and relax for a few minutes. Reflect on each goal with which you worked in this exercise.

- Of what was I aware as I worked on unblocking each goal (thoughts, feelings, images)?
- How am I seeing each goal differently?
- What new insights do I have?

Reenacting Your Life's Journey

Getting Started

You will need a room that is relatively free of obstruction because you will be moving around. You will probably want to work alone or with a friend. Make sure you will not be interrupted. You will probably need about one and a half hours. Choose a favorite piece of classical music to use in the exercise.

Basic Process

Begin by remembering as many events, people, places, and things from your life as you can. Then you will create a time line that will give you a picture of your life to the present. Finally, you will imagine that you have gone back to various stages of your past and will reenact these stages, gleaning wisdom from them for your future.

Exercise 1: Creating the Initial Time Line

Get a copy of a time line from your teacher.

- ◆ Divide your current age by three and divide the section of the time line labeled "Year" into this number of segments. Draw the dividing lines to the bottom of the chart, through the section called "Key Events." Number each segment with the three-year span that is appropriate, starting with the year of your birth, for example, 1986–1989, 1990–1993, 1993–1996.

- ◆ For each segment, brainstorm events you remember from that time of your life and list them in the "Key Events" section. Try to recall three to five things for each segment. Exact dates are not important. You're after general impressions.

- ◆ Look over these events and see if you can divide your life into a series of two to three distinct stages. Don't worry about being precise. Let your intuition be your guide.

- ◆ Make up a title that briefly describes each stage of your life and write the titles in the appropriate spaces.

Exercise 2: Exploring Your Time Line through Movement

Move to a part of the room where you have some space and can move about freely. You will need to have your time line nearby in case you need to refer to it. Choose a favorite piece of classical music and play it during the next stage of this practice.

- ◆ Close your eyes and take several deep breaths. Listen to the music and allow yourself to become relaxed, centered, and balanced.

- ◆ As vividly as you can, imagine that you have journeyed back to the first stage of your life. Review the events and begin moving around the space in ways that embody what this stage was like for you. As fully as you can, reenact this stage of your life for at least five minutes.

- ◆ When you feel that you have fully explored this first stage, proceed to the second stage. Again, taking at least five minutes, reenact this stage of your life's journey.

- ◆ Continue this process for each stage of your life's journey.

- ◆ When you have reenacted your entire life up to the present, stop and close your eyes. Take several deep breaths, relax, and become very focused and centered.

- ◆ In your imagination only, return to the first phase of your life and remember what you did to reenact or embody that stage. Try to experience yourself doing the movements again, but this time only in your mind.

- ◆ Continue moving through each stage of your life in your imagination only, trying to recontact some of the feelings, energy, and wisdom that you expressed when you were actually moving your body.

- ◆ When you have completed the journey, take several deep breaths and relax, listening to the music for a few moments. Open your eyes and return to the space where you created your time line.

Exercise 3: Harvesting the Results of the Exercise

Use the chart on page 12 to help you reflect on your experience of reenacting your life's journey. Divide the chart into the appropriate number of columns for the stages on your time line.

Kinesthetic Body Awareness

If You Can Think, Feel, and Do It, You Can Become It!

Contemporary researchers often talk about the "kinesthetic" body—the body of muscular imagination. There are many everyday examples of this special body. People who have lost a limb will often continue to experience sensations as if the limb were still there. Dancers, actors, and athletes often practice their skills many times with their physical body and then, with equal seriousness and rigor, practice them with the kinesthetic body.

Getting Acquainted with Your Kinesthetic Body*

Getting Started

For the first two exercises, you will need to work alone or with a partner. Find a space where you have some room to move around. Give yourself at least forty-five minutes of uninterrupted time for each exercise.

*Adapted from Houston, J. 1982. *The Possible Human* (Los Angeles: J.P. Tarcher) and from Lazear, David. 1991. *Seven Ways of Knowing: Understanding Multiple Intelligences* (Palatine, Ill.: Skylight).

Name of Stage	
What movements did I use to express this stage and why?	
What strikes me about this stage?	
What feelings has this exercise evoked in me?	
What did I learn about this stage of my life? What new insights have I gained?	
What did I learn from this stage of my life that needs to be part of my life today?	

Look for any themes that seem to run through the stages of your journey. On the top row of your time line, create a title for your whole life up to the present. Make it like the title of a movie, a miniseries, or a novel. What do you think might be in store for you in the next stage of your life?

Intelligence Builders for Every Student © 1998 Zephyr Press, Tucson, AZ

Exercise 1: Basic Awareness of Your Kinesthetic Body (simple)

1. Stand in a comfortable position and close your eyes. Focus on your breathing for a few minutes to help you relax and get centered.

2. Mentally scan your body, moving from your feet to the top of your head: What are the feelings and sensations in each part of your body? Are you equally aware of all parts of your body? Are some parts difficult to sense? Make a mental note about everything you are feeling and observing in your body; at the end of the following exercises, you will compare your body awareness then with your awareness now.

3. Keep your eyes closed, and paying full attention, slowly raise your right hand over your head and stretch your arm. If you are left-handed, raise your left hand. What muscles are involved and how do they move? What happens to the alignment of your body? What do your shoulders do? Your chest? Your hands and fingers? Your head? Your legs?

4. Lower your arm and again watch and feel everything that goes on in your body (answer the same questions as in step 3). How is it different and how is it the same as raising the arm?

5. Raise and lower your arm over and over again, each time trying to become more aware of what goes on in your body.

6. When you feel that you know intimately every detail of what goes on in this process, repeat the same process with your kinesthetic body: imagine that you are raising your hand over your head and stretching your arm. Try to experience the total process in your imagination as vividly and with as much reality as when you were doing it with your physical arm. Answer the three questions in step 3.

7. Do the exercise again with your physical arm, then with your kinesthetic arm. Go back and forth between the physical and kinesthetic arms until your experiences are almost identical.

8. Repeat the entire process with your other arm. Then repeat the process raising both arms at the same time.

9. Stop and rest for a few moments, reflecting on what this exercise was like for you. Then, if possible, proceed immediately to the next exercise.

Exercise 2: Amplified Awareness of Your Kinesthetic Body (complex)

Try each of the following miniexercises in turn. They will allow you to explore the kinesthetic body.

Physical and Kinesthetic Momentum

1. Stand in a comfortable position and close your eyes. Paying full attention circle your arms and shoulders forward. Feel the forward momentum of your arms and shoulders.

2. Stop circling your physical arms and shoulders but continue with your kinesthetic arms and shoulders. See if you can continue to feel the

momentum in your kinesthetic body. Again circle with your physical arms and shoulders, then stop and continue with your kinesthetic arms and shoulders.

3. Keep going back and forth between the physical experience and the kinesthetic experience until you almost cannot tell the difference between them.

4. Stop and rest for a few minutes, reflecting on this experience.

Physical and Kinesthetic Opposites

1. Focus your attention on your physical arms hanging at your sides. Slowly raise them, reaching for the sky, and hold them there. At the same time see if you can feel your kinesthetic arms hanging at your sides.

2. Slowly lower your physical arms while raising your kinesthetic arms, reaching for the sky. When you have a sense of how this movement feels, lower your kinesthetic arms while you raise your physical arms over your head. The key here is to pay full attention to the kinesthetic movements as you do to the movements with your physical arms.

3. Keep practicing this movement until the raising and lowering of your kinesthetic arms becomes almost indistinguishable from the raising and lowering of your physical arms. Can you sense the moment when the two sets of arms pass each other?

4. Stop and rest for a couple of minutes, reflecting on this movement.

Physical and Kinesthetic Total Body Movement

1. Continue to stand in a relaxed and centered position, breathing deeply, but open your eyes.

2. Being very mindful of what you are doing, mentally prepare your body; with your feet together jump forward about two or three feet, then jump back, paying close attention to the feel of your body in motion.

3. When you feel you have a strong sense of these movements, stop jumping with the physical body but continue jumping with your kinesthetic body, trying to experience the motion of the kinesthetic body as vividly as you did the movement of the physical body. Alternate between the physical and kinesthetic body until you can't tell the difference between them.

4. Pause and rest for a couple of minutes.

Uniting the Physical and Kinesthetic Bodies

1. Mentally prepare your body for action, then jump forward with your physical body and try to sense your kinesthetic body standing behind you.

2. Jump back with your physical body while you jump forward with your kinesthetic body. Reverse the actions, jumping forward with your physical body while you jump backward with your kinesthetic body. Keep jumping until you almost have a sense of the two bodies passing in midair!

3. When your kinesthetic body is forward and your physical body is back, stop. With your physical body, jump forward into the kinesthetic body. Stand very still, close your eyes for a few minutes, and notice how you feel. Do you have a greater awareness of your body now? Can you sense the two bodies as one? What do you notice about how your sense of your body has changed? What is going on in your emotions? What are you feeling? Can you feel the physical body and the kinesthetic body as one?

4. Open your eyes and walk around the space. See if your perceptions of your surroundings have changed.

Spend a few minutes reflecting on what you learned about yourself and your body as you worked back and forth between your physical body and your kinesthetic body.

The Kinesthetic Body in Everyday Life*

Getting Started

Read each of the following exercises. The first exercise may be an easier entry point, but you may begin with either exercise according to your needs. I suggest that you first master the exercises of "Getting Acquainted with Your Kinesthetic Body" before you try these.

Basic Process

The exercise asks you to consider your personal life and to work on improving various skills. You may notice instant changes; however, if you don't, do not get discouraged. Just keep working at it.

Exercise 1: Using the Kinesthetic Body in Your Personal Life

Try the following miniexercises and see if you can find ways to use the kinesthetic body to improve your performance in your everyday life.

Everyday "Body Stuff"

1. Brainstorm a list of seven to ten physical activities that you commonly do. Try for a range, including things that you enjoy, things at which you are very skilled, things that need a lot of improvement. Consider such activities as doing a hobby, exercising, playing a sport, dancing, walking in the park, and playing a musical instrument.

---

*Exercises in this section are adapted from Houston, J. 1982. *The Possible Human* (Los Angeles: J.P. Tarcher) and Lazear, David. 1991. *Seven Ways of Knowing: Understanding Multiple Intelligences* (Palatine, Ill.: Skylight).

2. Choose an activity in which you feel very skilled but in which there is also room for improvement. Do the activity, paying full attention to everything your physical body does—the muscles involved, the mind-body connection, the alignment of your body.

3. Pause for a moment and reflect on what parts of this performance you can improve. Close your eyes and perform the activity again, this time in your kinesthetic body only. See if you can kinesthetically do the activity to perfection.

4. Do it again in your physical body, trying to embody what you learned and observed in your kinesthetic performance. Go back and forth between the physical rehearsal and the kinesthetic rehearsal until you sense a shift in the performance of your physical body.

5. Briefly reflect on what happened in this miniexercise: surprises? interesting observations? discoveries? other things you want to try?

Using the Kinesthetic Body to Train the Physical Body

1. Choose an activity that is important to you and in which you are not so skilled.

2. Do the activity, paying full attention to everything your physical body does—the muscles involved, the mind-body connection, and so on.

3. Pause for a moment and reflect on the aspects of your performance that need improvement.

4. Close your eyes and imagine a master of the skill performing the activity. As vividly as you can, visualize this person's every move. Replay this visualization several times in slow motion until you have a clear mental picture of everything that is involved in the exemplary performance of the skill. Notice such things as posture, alignment of the body, the precision of each movement.

5. Continuing to visualize this master, engage your kinesthetic body and perform the skill with the master, mimicking the movements precisely in your kinesthetic body. Keep working until you have mastered the skill in your kinesthetic body.

6. Perform the skill with your physical body. Stop, close your eyes, and perform it with your kinesthetic body, comparing your kinesthetic mastery with the performance of your physical body. Again perform it with your physical body, incorporating the mastery of your kinesthetic body into the performance of your physical body.

7. Keep working back and forth between the kinesthetic body and the physical body until you feel that you are experiencing some level of improvement in your physical performance of the skill.

8. Stop and rest for a few minutes. Briefly reflect on your experience of this miniexercise: surprises? interesting observations? discoveries? other things you want to try?

Expanding Awareness through and throughout the Body

How Does the Body Pull It Off?

> *The body is a source of deep wisdom and understanding.*

Expanding Awareness *through* the Body

Getting Started

For this practice you will need to be alone or work with a partner. You will also need a block of uninterrupted time and a space that is relatively quiet and free of external distractions.

Basic Process

The exercises that follow work with a variety of so-called automatic body responses and movements. The first starts with relatively simple, one-dimensional tasks. The second exercise moves to more complex, multidimensional tasks. The third exercise works with movements that are more subtle. You will probably find it most useful to do the exercises in sequence, since each assumes the body wisdom of the previous exercise.

Exercise 1: Awareness of "Simple" Tasks

Dressing

1. Put on a jacket. Think your way through the process of taking it off. See if you can recall every distinct movement you will have to make to remove the jacket.

2. Actually take off the jacket. What did you leave out when you were only thinking about taking it off?

3. Put the jacket back on and try the exercise again. Repeat this process until you have brought your mental awareness more in line with the body's actual movements.

Walking

1. Go for a walk, walking in a fairly brisk manner. Try to pay attention to the process of your walking, seeing if you can figure out everything that is involved in this activity.

2. Continue walking, but cut your speed in half. Observe the process of your walking. What new aspects of how you walk are you aware of?

3. Continue walking, but in slow motion. Observe the process again and notice what you didn't notice before. Try to understand fully how the body does this activity.

4. Continue walking, slowly increasing your speed until you are again walking briskly. Try to maintain the same level of awareness as when you were walking in slow motion. If you lose the awareness, slow down until you regain it, then speed up gradually.

Exercise 2: Awareness of More Complex Tasks

Physical Exercise

1. Choose a physical exercise that is fairly easy for you, for example, jumping jacks, push-ups, or jogging. Think your way through doing the activity.

2. Perform the activity and compare what you actually do with your mental awareness of it. Keep doing the activity until you feel that you know everything that the body does.

3. Stop and rest. See if you can think your way through doing the activity, then do it again. Repeat the process until what you actually do is at least 90 percent accurate of the "thinking through."

Catching a Thrown Object

1. Ask a partner to throw an object to you twenty-five times. Each time, try to increase your awareness of everything that is involved, for example, your partner's intention to throw; the object in the air; the initial, subtle movement of your muscles as well as the gross movement of reaching for the object.

2. Stop and see if you can remember how you caught the object. Can you recall everything involved in the process? Talk to your partner about the action, then have her throw the object several more times, noticing what you forgot.

3. Go back and forth between the mental and physical processes, until you remember at least 90 percent of the actions.

Intelligence Builders for Every Student © 1998 Zephyr Press, Tucson, AZ

Exercise 3: Awareness of More Subtle Tasks

The Relaxation Process

1. Take yourself through the process of your favorite technique for relaxing, or experiment with one of the following: tense then suddenly release the muscles of the lower body, then the upper body; breathe slowly and deeply for ten minutes; move your awareness slowly from your toes to the top of your head, systematically relaxing each set of muscles; take a hot bath or a hot tub or jacuzzi; get a full-body massage; listen to soothing music; find a quiet place in nature where you can lie down and let yourself go

2. Pay close attention to what your body does when it wants to relax. Can you distinguish among the different phases of the process? What part of the process is more-or-less automatic, and what takes some conscious effort? What have you learned from doing this miniexercise that you could use to help you reduce the stress in your daily life?

Expanding Awareness *throughout* the Body

Getting Started

For the following exercise you will need to be alone or work with a partner. You will also need a block of uninterrupted time and a space that is relatively quiet and free of distractions.

Basic Process

The first exercise deals with a powerful technique developed by Mathis Alexander called the "STOP technique." This technique teaches you to experience your whole body and to expand your awareness of living throughout the whole body. The second exercise works more directly with understanding the perceptual feedback the body is continually providing. Do the exercises in sequence.

Exercise 1: Enhancing Body Awareness (simple)*

1. Go outdoors to a favorite place where you have plenty of space for walking. Begin walking briskly around this space. After about two minutes, **STOP.** Focus on the bottoms of your feet. How do they feel?

2. Walk again, trying to stay aware of the bottoms of your feet. How are they involved in your walking? How do they feel when you are walking as opposed to when you were simply standing?

3. After another two minutes or so, **STOP.** Add to your awareness of the bottoms of your feet an awareness of your legs. How do they feel?

4. Start walking again, trying to stay aware of the bottoms of your feet and your legs. How are the legs involved in your walking? How do they feel when you are walking as opposed to when you were simply standing? Be careful. Don't lose awareness of the bottoms of your feet as you pay attention to your legs!

*Adapted from Lazear, David. 1991. *Seven Ways of Knowing: Teaching for Multiple Intelligences* (Palatine, Ill.: Skylight).

5. After another two minutes, **STOP.** Continue to add this process to different parts of your body (the hips, the arms and shoulders, the torso, and the neck and head). Each time use this process: **STOP** and focus on a "new" part of the body; note how it feels. Walk again for two minutes; try to maintain the previous awareness plus the involvement of the "new" body part. **STOP** and add awareness of another part.

   Note: When you lose awareness of a body part, **STOP** and back up to the point where it was clear for you. Start walking again until you have regained clarity, then add the new part.

6. Pause and rest for a few minutes. Reflect on what it was like to extend awareness throughout the body: What did you notice? How does it feel to have activated this kind of awareness? What have you learned about yourself and your body?

Exercise 2: Enhancing Body Awareness (complex)

1. Repeat exercise 1 until you are able to walk with full body awareness without losing the awareness of any part.

2. **STOP.** Add the awareness of the sounds in the environment, including the sound of your walking. Start walking again, trying to maintain the awareness of your whole body while you also pay attention to sound.

3. After two minutes, **STOP.** One by one add awareness of each of the remaining senses (sight, smell, taste, and touch). Each time you add a new sense, make sure that you don't lose awareness of another sense.

   Note: When you lose the awareness of one aspect of the body or one of the senses, **STOP** and return to the point in your walking where these aspects were clear. Start walking again until you have regained clarity, then systematically add the new aspects.

4. Pause and rest for a few minutes. Reflect on what it was like to extend awareness throughout the body: What did you notice? How does it feel to have activated this kind of awareness? What have you learned about your self and your body?

Exercise 3: The Body as a Radar Station (listening to the body)

External Stimuli

1. Next time you experience one of the following, pause and notice how your body is involved: you hear a favorite song playing; you see something that repulses you; you smell a favorite food cooking; you hear a sound that startles you; you touch something that pleases you; you see another person who is special to you; you taste something you dislike; you read something with which you disagree.

2. Keep a journal or reflective diary for two or three weeks. Log your observations of your body's responses. See if you can learn to listen to your body as carefully as you listen to your mind.

Intelligence Builders for Every Student © 1998 Zephyr Press, Tucson, AZ

3. Brainstorm ways your body gives you feedback that could help you live more effectively, for example, knowing when you've had enough to eat, or knowing how to lift something heavy.

The Emotions and the Body

1. Next time you experience a strong emotional response to something, pause for a moment and notice how your body is involved. For example, how does your body respond to each of the following emotions: joy, anger, anxiety, peace, irritation with someone else, surprise, impatience, depression, contentment, boredom, excitement, fear, amusement?

2. Keep a journal or reflective diary for two weeks. Carefully log your observations of your bodily-kinesthetic responses to emotional experiences. See if you can discover various physical patterns that are present when you are angry, for example, or when you experience joy.

3. Experiment with using the body to help you shift and manage your emotions. For example, when you notice the "stress response" occurring, intentionally shift your body to the physical patterns you observed for the "at-peace response," or shift your body from the "irritation response" to the "amused response." Try various combinations of emotions and postures that you think will help you gain a greater control over your emotions.

Watching a Movie or TV Show

1. Next time you are watching a movie or a TV show, watch yourself watching. Notice how your body responds to what is happening on the screen. For example, how does your body respond when there is a lot of suspense? Something bad happens to a character you really like? The show is very amusing? A character you hate appears? You see obvious injustice? A passionate love scene occurs? There is a chase scene? A violent act occurs? The plot moves slowly? There is a surprise ending or an unanticipated development? Watch for both very obvious, big physical responses as well as the more subtle ones, such as sweaty palms, increased heart rate, and dryness in the mouth.

List times in your everyday life when your body makes similar responses to situations. Reflect on what it would mean to really listen to your body in these situations.

Mind-Body Connection

Your Body Knows. Do You?

> *This practice works with the relationship between the mind and the body. One of the most interesting findings of contemporary brain-mind research is that the brain cannot distinguish the difference between something that is vividly and actively imagined and physical reality. You can produce real physiological changes in the body simply by altering what is going on in your mind.*

Mind-Body Connection Practice

Getting Started

Each exercise can be integrated easily into your daily routine; however, each also requires some time for reflection and for planning for different kinds of experiments with the mind-body connection.

Basic Process

Do these exercises in sequence.

Exercise 1: Ordinary Mind-Body Connections*

1. Close your eyes and, as vividly as you can, imagine the following things. *Pay attention to the effect each has on your body:* the sound of fingernails or chalk scraping on a blackboard; the taste of a lemon; the taste of your favorite dessert; the feel of a newborn baby; the smell of someone smoking a cigar.

2. Close your eyes and again, as vividly as you can, imagine yourself in the following situations. *Pay attention to the effect each imagined scene has on your body:* you are walking down a dark street at night and sense you are being followed; you are sunbathing on a secluded tropical beach, listening to the ocean waves; you are sitting in a meeting where someone is expressing an opinion with which you violently disagree.

*Adapted from Lazear, David. 1991. *Seven Ways of Knowing: Understanding Multiple Intelligences* (Palatine, Ill.: Skylight).

3. Finally, reflect on what you have discovered about how what is in the mind affects the body. What strikes you? What patterns have you observed? What do you find especially interesting? Surprising? Distressing? Amusing? What have you discovered about yourself? What other areas of the mind-body connection do you want to explore (for example, the physiological effect of certain emotionally charged words or phrases or the effect of visual or auditory stimuli)?

Exercise 2: Listening to Feedback from Your Mind and Body

1. Use the chart to help you become aware of the kinds of mind and body responses to various situations. Log at least one experience for each category. Use the descriptive categories to analyze further.

	Anxiety	Joy	Excitement	Contentment	Stress	Other
Situation I was in						
What I noticed going on in my mind						
What I noticed going on in my body						

2. Reflect on the chart. What immediately grabs your attention? What strikes you? What do you see that surprises you? Intrigues you? Distresses you? Where do you see direct correlations between what was going on in your body and what was going on in your mind?

Exercise 3: Reprogramming Mind-Body Connections

1. In this exercise you will be planning various strategies to help you deal effectively with daily negative situations. Start with the chart you filled out in exercise 2. Focus on the "Anxiety" or the "Stress" column. Plan mind-body strategies you could use to help you deal more effectively with a stressful situation.

2. Construct a four-column chart with the headings *Emotional Response* (How am I feeling?), *Situation* (What are the external circumstances?), *Body Response* (What goes on in my body?), and *Mind Response* (What goes on in my mind?). List at least three more negative emotional responses you frequently experience during a normal day, for example, boredom, anger, apathy, helplessness, low self-esteem, and a desire for revenge. Then fill in the information in the other columns.

3. Plan a series of mind-body strategies you can use to help you deal more effectively with each situation you have listed.

4. At the end of each day, write your reflections on what you have learned about yourself. What do you remember from your experiments with your mind-body connections today? What surprised you? Annoyed you? Intrigued you? Excited you? What did you learn about yourself? What new insights have you gained? What new strategies do you want to try tomorrow?

Interpersonal Intelligence

Improving Group Processing Skills

Getting Our Act Together So We Can Take It on the Road!

> This practice develops the social skills needed for effective human relating and collaborating. Real listening is a complex skill that takes practice.

Phase 1: An Inventory of Personal Social Skills

Getting Started

You need help from someone you trust and who trusts you, with whom you can be very honest and open.

Basic Process

The first exercise asks you to evaluate your own social skills, and the second exercise asks your friend to evaluate your skills. Follow exercise 1 immediately with exercise 2.

Exercise 1: Analysis of the Self

1. You and your partner rank yourselves on a scale of 1 to 5 for each skill listed (5 = highly skilled, 4 = shows promise, 3 = average, 2 = needs work, 1 = trouble area). Don't share the results of your inventory yet.

Personal Social Skills

listens when another is talking	finds points of agreement
carries own weight	is sensitive to others' moods and feelings
assists others	clarifies things that are confusing
includes everyone	paraphrases ideas
supports and encourages others	gives examples
respects others' opinions	probes for differences
helps group stay focused	generates alternatives
allows and encourages participation	elaborates on ideas and extends group's
keeps an open mind	thinking
disagrees with ideas, not people	integrates ideas
sees all points of view	helps group reach consensus

2. When both of you have finished the inventory, individually relist the skills from the inventory in the appropriate columns of the following chart.

5 Highly Skilled	**4** Shows Promise	**3** Average	**2** Needs Work	**1** Trouble Area

3. Spend a moment *individually* reflecting on the the items in each column. What strikes you immediately? What did you expect? What surprises you? What connections do you see within a column?

Exercise 2: Analysis of the Self by Another

1. Repeat the inventory, this time evaluating each other. Use the same scale you used to evaluate yourselves.

2. When both of you have finished the inventories, individually relist the skills from the inventory in the appropriate columns of the chart.

3. Share your self-evaluation charts and the charts you did for each other. Compare these and discuss those areas where you differ.

4. Together, brainstorm at least ten practical strategies for each of you to improve your skills. ***Remember, your goal is to help each other strengthen these interpersonal skills.***

Phase 2: Group Dynamics and Processing Skills

Getting Started

In these exercises you analyze a group of which you are a part. Although you can do the exercises on your own, you will probably find them easier and more interesting if you work with one or two other group members.

Basic Process

In the first exercise you analyze the interactions of a group and create a plan for improving the effectiveness of those interactions. The second exercise asks you to implement group processing practices to help the group become more aware of its dynamics.

Exercise 1: Analysis of a Group

1. Select a group of which you are an active member. Evaluate the group over the course of several formal meetings by listing the following and writing whether your group is excellent, okay, or does not yet practice each skill.

   has a clear mission
   shares responsibility for work
   varies group meeting times and dates
   deals with diversity
   celebrates together
   has identity symbols (for example, logo, song)
   shares leadership
   inspires involvement
   seeks group consensus
   enjoys one another's company
   manages conflict
   welcomes new members
   listens to one another
   supports and encourages one another
   other

2. After completing the chart, list the items in the appropriate columns on a chart with the columns *Excellent, Okay,* and *Not Yet.*

Items Marked "Excellent"	Items Marked "Okay"	Items Marked "Not Yet"

3. With your partners, discuss your evaluation, reflecting on the following questions: What is the first thing you notice? What do you see that surprises you? What does not surprise you? What interests you most? What confuses you? What seems contradictory? Do you see any patterns within the columns? What connections do you see within a column? What connections do you see among various columns?

4. Analyze the chart for areas that need to be improved. Stay focused on group processes. Don't get lost in individual personality issues or your personal feelings. Look for such things as unclear procedures, structural problems, confusing or contradictory policies, organizational issues.

5. Finally, write a one-sentence description of each problem area and five practical skills to improve it.

6. Keep a log of things the group tries and the results you see. Don't give up. Remember that a group is organic. Use the original evaluation form to help you recognize the changes and growth. Continue to plan new strategies that foster higher levels of effective group process.

Exercise 2: Group Processing Reflection

1. Select a group of which you are an active member. Request a time to share the evaluation list.

2. Pass out copies of the list to the members and ask them to quickly rank the group. Use a scale of 1 to 3, where 3 means "We're exemplary—other groups could learn from us"; 2 means "We're okay but nothing to write home about"; and 1 means "Uh-oh! We've got some work to do!" Encourage them to go with their first impressions.

3. Collect the checklists and tell the group you will present the results at the next meeting. Work with your partners to compile the data. Total the numbers for each item and divide by the number of checklists completed.

4. Chart each item 2.5–3, 1.5–2.4, 0–1.4.

5. At the next meeting, explain how the data were compiled and present the chart. Explain that this chart simply tallies *their* responses to the checklist—it is not your opinion of how the group functions. Also, explain that the point of this exercise is to help the group improve its processing skills.

6. Discuss the chart using the following questions: What is the first thing you notice? What surprises you? What does not surprise you? What is most interesting? What is confusing or contradictory? What patterns do you see within a column? What connections do you see among columns?

7. For each column, brainstorm several things the group could experiment with to strengthen their skills. For the "Exemplary" column, ask, "What can we do to undergird these items? Also, can we use any of these items to help us work on improving skills in the other columns?" For the "Okay" column, ask, "What steps could we take to make these items exemplary?" For the "Uh-Oh" column, ask, "What are some new things we could try that might help us face the issues and challenges in this column?"

Positive Interdependence

I'll Do My Thing! You Do Your Thing! Then Just Look at the Group Thing!

> *Probably the most important factor in the success of any team is positive interdependence. Sports teams are the clearest illustration of this. Each player has a specific task to perform, and the success of the team depends on each player performing well.*

Phase 1: Positively Linked for Success

Getting Started

You need the help of several friends who are interested in developing their interpersonal intelligences. Each exercise requires planning, so you need to read the procedures first.

Basic Process

These exercises build your capacity for complex positive interdependence. Exercise 1 asks you to draw something with a partner. Exercise 2 has you build something with two other people. Exercise 3 is collaborative writing with at least two other people.

Exercise 1: Draw This!

1. Work with a partner. First, each of you draws a relatively simple geometric pattern. Don't show the drawings to each other yet.

2. Decide who will be the describer and who the drawer. The describer gives only oral descriptions to get the drawer to reproduce the design. The drawer tries to draw the design accurately. The describer may say anything but may not look at what the drawer is drawing. The drawer may ask questions, but the drawer may not look at the describer's drawing until both feel they have successfully completed the drawing.

3. Spend a few minutes reflecting on your experience by answering the following questions: What did you do that helped? What was confusing? What could you have done that might have helped more? What strategies should you try when you reverse roles?

4. Switch roles and repeat the process.

5. Try the exercise several times to improve your performance. How "in synch" with your partner can you get? You may want to vary the exercise, increasing the difficulty and tapping into some of your extraordinary interpersonal capacities. Try imposing a time limit and see how quickly you can successfully reproduce the designs. Create increasingly complex designs. Add color to the designs.

Exercise 2: Build This!*

1. You need two friends. One of you is the builder, one the question-asker, and one the answer-giver. Decide among you who will play which role.

2. The answer-giver builds something using Tinker Toys, building blocks, or Legos and places the product behind a screen. He or she then places pieces identical to those used in the building in a bag. The goal is for the builder to replicate the object behind the screen without looking at it or talking to others on the team.

3. The answer-giver looks at the construction behind the screen. She may not speak and may not help the builder in any direct way by touching or pointing to the construction pieces. The question-asker asks the answer-giver questions about the construction. He may ask *only* yes-or-no questions of the answer-giver. He may not look at the construction; however, the question-asker may give oral instructions to the builder. The builder follows the question-asker's instructions as faithfully as possible. The builder may not talk.

4. Discuss your experience, noting what you did that helped one another and what you could do to help more. Try the exercise again and see if you can improve your performance. You may change roles and see how that alters the exercise.

Exercise 3: Write This!

1. You need at least two other people. Begin by brainstorming a list of at least twenty topics about which various members of the group would like to write.

2. Select one item that interests the whole group.

3. Decide together on the most appropriate genre for the topic (story, essay, persuasive speech, formal report, letter, poem). Decide who will write first, who will write second, and so on.

4. Appoint a timekeeper. The first person writes for two minutes and introduces the topic. The second person reads the composition aloud, then writes for two minutes. The third person reads the entire composition aloud, then writes for two minutes.

5. Repeat the process until each person has read aloud and written twice.

Reflect on the exercises by answering the following questions: What was your experience? What happened among you and your partners? What really struck you? Which of the exercises was most interesting? Most surprising? Most challenging? Most fun?

*Adapted from Lazear, David. 1991. *Seven Ways of Knowing: Teaching for Multiple Intelligences* (Palatine, Ill.: Skylight).

What did you learn about your interpersonal capacities by doing these exercises? What areas are strong? What areas do you need to strengthen? What did you learn about your partners? What did you learn from them?

Phase 2: Positively Linked for Learning

Getting Started

Do the exercises with a group that already exists or ask a group of friends to do them with you. You need about four or five people.

Basic Process

In the first exercise you participate in cooperative learning. In the second exercise, your group creates a product.

Exercise 1: Each One Teach One

1. Pair off. Each person makes a secret list of five to seven things she can teach her partner (for example, a magic trick, a poem, a computer operation, a song).

2. The pairs exchange lists and each person selects one item from the partner's list. Partners discuss what helps each of them learn—visual aids, written steps, and so on.

3. Each person takes a few minutes to plan a teaching strategy.

4. Each person teaches his partner the chosen skill, making sure to assess whether or not the other person masters it. If more teaching is needed, this is the time to do it.

5. When each pair has successfully mastered the selected items, each person chooses a new partner and teaches that person what she just learned. The new pairs discuss what helps them learn and take a few minutes to plan their teaching strategies.

6. Teach and then assess.

7. The whole group reflects on the exercise using the following questions: What are some of the things you learned? What did you notice about the process? What did you learn about working with a partner? What was fun? What was difficult? What was exciting? What was surprising? When have you experienced this one-on-one teaching in other situations? When and where in everyday life do you need the skills called for? What could you do to improve your performance?

Exercise 2: The Cooperative Learning Jigsaw

1. Work in groups of four. Assign the following roles to members of the group: organizer (keeps group moving and on task), cheerleader (encourages the group), timekeeper (ensures the activity happens within time parameters), and checker (checks for understanding).

2. The organizer leads the group in brainstorming items the group wants or needs to learn about. Select the item that interests people the most and that all are willing to learn.

3. Agree on an equitable way to divide the material among all members. Each person studies her piece and figures out how to teach it so that all members master it. Agree on the time needed. The timekeeper watches the clock and adjusts the time for individual team members, if necessary. Encourage people to use a variety of techniques.

4. At the end of the time, the timekeeper calls the group together. Decide how much time each person needs to teach his part. Each member gives a presentation, allowing for questions and discussion as needed.

5. After the presentations, the checker quizzes the group and reviews any parts they have not mastered.

6. The organizer leads the group to reflect on this cooperative learning experience: What parts of the process impressed you the most? When were you excited? When were you anxious? What surprised you? What disturbed you? What other feelings did you have and when? What parts of the process did you do well? What strategies did you use that helped each person succeed? If you were to do this exercise again, what would you change? What could you do that would enhance, deepen, or expand the effectiveness of your collaborative skills? Brainstorm a list of other situations where you could use this cooperative learning process.

Phase 3: Positively Linked for Decision Making

Getting Started

This practice will be most effective with an existent group. Introduce the consensus-forming process when the group is planning a course of action or making a difficult decision, especially when there are differing opinions. You need one member of the group to be the facilitator, and you need these supplies: large index cards, one broad-tipped marker per person, masking tape, and a flip chart.

Basic Process

After you select an issue, each member thinks about it before you begin. The group works on understanding the common areas and the areas of disagreement. Finally, you work on forging a consensus.

The following instructions are for the facilitator:

1. Lead the group in brainstorming a list of ten items about which a decision must be made. Choose an issue that your group is really facing. If no such issues exist, choose something such as planning a party or a potential fund-raiser.

2. As a group, choose an item to focus on. Write the issue as a question on a large sheet of paper and post it where all can see it. Work with the group to state the question as clearly as possible.

3. Ask the group to brainstorm individually a list of ten ideas related to the focus question.

4. Ask each person to choose a partner and share lists. Pass out a stack of index cards and two markers to each pair. As they consider each other's lists, the pairs decide on seven to ten of their best, most creative ideas and write these on cards. Ask them to write large and to try to state each idea in a three- to five-word phrase. Have them put masking tape on the back of each card.

5. Ask each pair to select the three cards that they believe have the clearest ideas. Collect the three cards from each pair and stick them randomly on a wall, reading what is on each card.

6. Ask the group if any ideas need to be clarified; have the appropriate pair clarify. Then ask if any ideas should be paired because they are the same. Move these cards together. Try to get every card paired with at least one other card, but don't force it.

7. When the group is satisfied with the initial grouping, ask partners to look at their remaining cards and select two more ideas. Collect these cards and place them randomly on the wall, reading the ideas aloud.

8. Ask the group to find ideas that go together. The group may notice that some of the new ideas need to join existing pairs and some of the existing pairs need to be clustered. Try to get every card into an emerging cluster and to have five to seven cards in a cluster.

9. Work with the group to create a title for each cluster.

10. Ask the pairs to sort their remaining cards into the appropriate clusters.

11. Ask each pair to join another pair. Divide the clusters of cards among these groups. The groups discuss the title and make any necessary revisions so that the title accurately represents that cluster.

12. Each group cooperates to write a brief paragraph that summarizes the distinct ideas on the cluster. Groups write their paragraphs on large flip chart sheets so that the cards can be posted for all to see. Try to eliminate any overlapping ideas.

13. Each group presents its writing to the large group for discussion and revision of any points that do not accurately represent the common mind.

14. Discuss the next steps, making necessary assignments, planning a time line, and so on.

Deep Hearing, Listening, and Understanding

I Hear WHAT You Say.
Do I UNDERSTAND What It Means?

> *How often have you thought you clearly communicated something to someone you thought was listening, only to be surprised later that the person missed the intent of your communication? Hearing another's words is one thing. But hearing and listening to what the person is saying is another matter. Understanding the meaning of the speaking is a highly developed skill. The exercises in this practice work with several levels of the hearing, listening, and understanding process in everyday situations.*

The Art of Listening and Understanding

Getting Started

Read through each exercise and recruit the appropriate people. Exercise 1 requires you to encounter other people who have a perspective with which you disagree. You can execute exercise 2 through daily communication.

Basic Process

These exercises develop your listening and understanding skills. You deal with a viewpoint with which you disagree, with communication that seems confusing or contradictory, and with everyday communications.

Exercise 1: Listening When You Disagree*

1. Ask another person with whose viewpoint you strongly disagree to explain her viewpoint to you. Listen as deeply as you can to what the other person is saying, trying to understand where she is coming from. Consciously practice cutting off the mind chatter (mental comments, such as about the person's clothing, planning your own rebuttal) that usually blocks genuine hearing.

*Adapted from Lazear, David. 1991. *Seven Ways of Knowing: Teaching for Multiple Intelligences* (Palatine, Ill.: Skylight).

2. When the person has finished, ask questions to clarify, but do not state your opinions. Remember that understanding is not the same as agreeing. Following are some questions to try, but be careful not to ask them in an argumentative way: Who are some people who have influenced your thinking? What experiences in your life have led to your current viewpoint? What are the most common arguments against your viewpoint and how do you answer them? Are there any books or articles you would recommend that would help me understand your position more fully?

3. Paraphrase what the other person has said and what her viewpoint on the issue is. Ask her to interrupt you and correct you if you have not fully understood what she was saying. At the end of the conversation, thank the person for sharing her views with you.

4. Immediately after the conversation, write a brief paragraph on how your own perspective has been informed.

Exercise 2: Listening When the Message Is Confusing

1. During the next month, whenever you are communicating with someone and you feel the message is unclear, you feel you are hearing contradictory information, you don't understand, or you feel the need to grasp the larger context, turn off the mind chatter. Listen as fully and deeply as you can, even though the communication is confusing. Do not accuse the other person of sending a confusing message. Do not look confused or communicate distress. Begin by saying to the other person, "I'm not sure I understand what you just said. What I heard you say was . . . " and repeat as accurately as you can what you heard.

2. Ask the person if you have heard correctly. If not, ask him to repeat the message. Note what parts of your confusion are cleared up. Zero in on those parts that are still confusing: Isolate the confusing and contradictory parts. In a nonaccusatory way, try to explain what is confusing or what seems contradictory, asking the other person to help you understand. Paraphrase what you heard and ask for confirmation or correction. Assess how the explanation has helped: What is still confusing? What still seems contradictory?

3. Immediately write a brief paragraph on your experience and what you learned about yourself. Also write about interpersonal skills you need to improve.

Seeing Yourself through Others' Eyes

What on Earth Does He/She See in Me?!

> *When we are with other people, we have certain perceptions that lead us to form opinions about the kind of people they must be. For example, we might see someone acting friendly and making witty remarks at a party, and we may assume she is very sure of herself and has many friends. Have you ever wondered how others perceive you and what assumptions they make about the kind of person you are?*

Phase 1: Seeing Yourself through Others' Eyes

Getting Started

The two exercises in this practice may take several weeks to complete. Don't let this time commitment discourage you—the benefits can be quite remarkable! Do the exercises at a comfortable pace that more or less fits into your daily routine.

Basic Process

The first exercise asks you to have conversations with people, then to analyze their perspectives of other people. The second exercise asks you to stand in their shoes and to share their perspectives of you.

Exercise 1: Discerning Others' Perspectives

1. Have conversations with several people about other people or human relationships in general. After each conversation, respond to the following questions for each person. What words and phrases give me clues to this person's opinions about other people and human relationships? When was I aware of this person's feelings about other people or human relationships? What do I sense are this person's core values and beliefs about other people or human relationships? What distinct ways of dealing with different kinds of people or relationships did this person express? Make a chart to summarize this information.

2. Reflect on the information you have recorded using the following questions: What immediately strikes me? What are my general observations? What surprises me most? What interests me most? What amuses me? Excites me? Disturbs me? Bores me? Mystifies me? What patterns do I see? What have I learned about these people?

Exercise 2: Discerning Others' Perspectives of You

1. Study the the chart in exercise 1. Pretend you are each person in turn and that you are having a conversation with another person about yourself. Answer the following questions for each category on the chart. Include direct and indirect feedback you have received from each person in the past in these areas. What key words/phrases would the person use to describe you? What feelings/ emotions about you would the person express? What values/beliefs about you would be supported or challenged as this person considers her relationship with you? What strategies/tactics would this person employ for dealing with you, given your imagined responses to the previous questions?

2. Read over the information on the charts and highlight the items that represent actual feedback. Reflect on this information by asking yourself the questions in step 2 of the first exercise.

3. List 3 to 5 things about how *you* perceive *others* perceive you that concern you.

Phase 2: Changing Others' Perspectives of You

1. Look over the concerns you listed at the end of exercise 2. Select those perceptions you want to alter. Use a chart with the headings *Areas of Concern, Current Behaviors* (that may reinforce inaccurate perceptions), and *New Behaviors* (that may contribute to more accurate perceptions), to help you think through things you might do to change another's perspective of you.

2. Create a time line for implementing the strategies. Give yourself plenty of time. Don't try to implement everything at once! You may find it useful to work on one concern at a time, or you may find that some of the strategies work on several areas of concern.

3. After a reasonable amount of time, evaluate the impact these strategies seem to be having on others' perspectives of you based on their direct and indirect feedback. List any changes you have observed in the same areas of perception you observed in exercise 1.

4. Using the same chart with which you worked in step 1, analyze your current behaviors and brainstorm new strategies at those points where you are still concerned or where the strategies you tried still aren't sending accurate messages about you to other people.

Mapping Personal Relationships

Getting to Know You, Getting to Know All about You

> *There is a mystery, depth, and greatness to every human being that often eludes us in our everyday relating to one another. Think about your fellow students. Do you really know what makes them tick?*

Creating Relationship Maps

Getting Started

For each exercise you need to select various people whom you know fairly well. You need three sheets of blank, preferably unlined, paper, and some fine-tipped marking pens in a variety of colors.

Basic Process

Each exercise uses *concept mapping.* A concept map starts with a central idea (in this case, a central relationship), then builds outward in a nonlinear fashion to help someone understand the idea (or relationship) more fully. You work alone to create the basic relationship map, then share your map with the appropriate person or persons.

Exercise 1: Mapping a Personal Relationship

1. Choose a person you know well and whom you trust. Each of you works alone to create a map of your relationship with each other.

2. Each write your two names at the center of a blank sheet of paper and circle them. Draw five lines out from the center circle. Discuss several defining aspects of your relationship and agree on at least five, for example, **qualities**, **shared experiences**, **hobbies**, **family members**, **beliefs or values**, and **activities**. Circle each of these.

3. *Working individually,* think about each aspect of the relationship. What thoughts, feelings, and experiences are sparked as you think about this relationship? What other dimensions of your relationship with this person do these circled items help you remember? Every time an association with the circled item comes to mind, make a line out from the item and record what you are thinking and feeling.

4. When you have finished your relationship map, write several sentences to complete the sentence: ***The significance of this relationship to me at this time in my life is . . .***

Intelligence Builders for Every Student © 1998 Zephyr Press, Tucson, AZ

5. Exchange maps. Study your partner's map for a few minutes. Reflect on the maps by asking each other the following questions: What was your first reaction to my map? What were your feelings as you studied it? What questions do you have about my map? Where do our maps reveal a common understanding? Where do we see some significant differences in our perception? What have we learned from doing the map? How else could we use this exercise to deepen and enhance our relationship?

Exercise 2: Mapping a Group or Organizational Relationship

1. Ask several people within a group to do this exercise with you. Make a concept map as you did in exercise 1, writing the name of your organization or club in the middle.

2. Get back together with your group members and exchange maps. Have each individual present her map. Reflect on the maps using the following questions: What immediately grabbed your attention? What items were expected? What were most surprising? What were your feelings as others were talking about their maps? What were your feelings as you were creating your own map? What questions do you have about any of the maps? Where do the maps reveal a common understanding? Where do you see some significant differences in your perception of the organization? How could you use this exercise to improve your organization?

Extending Personal Communication

Tell Me More!

Can you remember a time when someone told you something about herself and you wanted to know more, but you were afraid you would be prying? How about a time when you were sharing something with others and you wanted them to pry, but they didn't?

Phase 1: Going Beyond the Surface in Personal Communication

Getting Started

For the first exercise you need to work with a trusted friend. The second exercise requires you work with members of a group of which you are a part. You must be the group leader to do exercise 2.

Basic Process

Study the following discussion method. The first exercise asks you to apply the method in a dialogue, and the second exercise has you use it in a group.

Basic Discussion Method

Objective Questions: Begin with what people see, hear, touch, smell, and taste. This level tends to be verifiable by the five senses and by everyone involved in the discussion. When this level of a discussion is ignored, people interpret and make decisions based on erroneous information or subjective feelings only.

Reflective Questions: Illuminate what people feel toward something. This level is more personal. When this level of a discussion is ignored, people tend to remain dispassionate and make decisions void of commitment.

Interpretetive Questions: Highlight layers of meaning people ascribe to things, and the story out of which they will live in relation to it. When this level is ignored, outcomes and final decisions tend to be superficial.

Decisional Questions: Allow people to choose what they will do about a situation in light of the discussion. This level reveals people's decisions and the steps they plan to take. When this level is ignored, people generally leave feeling frustrated, for "all we did was talk and talk, but nothing was decided."

Exercise 1: Dialogue with One Other Person

1. Choose a partner. Together select a poem or an article from a magazine or newspaper that both of you find interesting. Read the poem or article aloud several times. What words or phrases grabbed you? Read the poem or article again and notice your feelings. What feelings did it call forth? What music would you play as a background for this poem or article? What colors does it evoke? If you could delete part of this poem or article, which part would it be? If you could add something, what would you add? If you could read this poem or article to anyone, to whom would you read it? Why? Try some word substitutions and see what that does to the poem or article. In your own words, what is the message of this poem or article? What real-life experience does it call to mind? When in your own experience have you known the truth of this poem or article? Tell each other about that time. Ask: If I gave you a nicely mounted copy of this poem or article, where would you hang it in your home? Why? If this poem or article were a person, what would you say to it?

Exercise 2: Dialogue with a Group

1. With a group of which you are a part, use the basic discussion method to discuss a movie you have seen together. What scenes do you remember? What sounds had an impact on you? What colors? What physical objects? What lines of dialogue are still ringing in your ears? Make a list of all the characters in the movie. Is there anyone you forgot to mention? Of the characters, whom did you like? Whom did you dislike? As you were watching the movie, when did you see emotion portrayed? When were you aware that you were responding

emotionally? What emotions did you feel? (Remember, you do not have to explain; just be aware.) When did the filmmakers use symbols? As you watched, what became a symbol for you? If you were to change anything about the movie, what would you change? If you had to tell someone in a couple of sentences what the movie was about, what would you say? In real life, where have you seen some of the things in the movie? What experiences in your life does this movie call to mind? With whom did you identify? Whom would you like to take to see this film? Why? If you had to give it a new title, what would it be?

Adapt the process to other situations, such as a book you have all read, a piece of art, a speech, a problem you are facing, or an important issue you're trying to sort through.

The Self Apart and the Self as a Part

No One Is an Island Entire unto the Self; We Are All Part of the Continent

> *Part of our self-understanding is our experience of being unique, apart from other people. However, often an even stronger part of our identity comes from our experience of being a part of the lives of other people, organizations, our country, and the world.*

The Self Apart and the Self as a Part*

Getting Started

You need no less than an hour and a half for these exercises. Choose a time when you can be alone and will not be interrupted. Before you start, gather the following supplies: three sheets of flip chart paper, broad-tipped marking pens in a variety of colors,

---

*Adapted from Houston, Jean. 1982. *The Possible Human* (Los Angeles: J. P. Tarcher) and
  Lazear, David. 1991. *Seven Ways of Knowing: Teaching for Multiple Intelligences* (Palatine, Ill.: Skylight).

three pieces of recorded music (something moderately paced with a definite beat, something "new age" that meanders and flows with no easily recognizable beat or melody, and largo or adagio baroque music), and a CD player or audiocassette player.

Basic Process

Do the exercises in sequence and in a single time period. Exercise 1 focuses on the individualistic self and exercise 2 focuses on the interpersonal self. The third exercise leads you through synthesizing these selves. Allow plenty of time for each exercise. Do not move to the next exercise until you have a feeling of completion of the preceding exercise.

Exercise 1: The Self Apart

1. Play a piece of moderately paced music that has a clear and definite beat, such as a march, something by Mozart or Stravinsky, or classical jazz. On a very large piece of unlined paper, using a broad-tipped marker, draw a human figure with boxes for the body, arms, and legs, and a circle for the head.

2. Inside the body box randomly list at least ten things you do individually, such as reading a book, watching TV, and doing your laundry.

3. For each activity you have written, draw a design, symbol, shape, or other visual image you associate with that activity. Use a variety of marking pens. Be creative and intuitive. Have fun.

4. Imagine that these items and drawings are in the inner workings of a very complex machine. Draw lines of connection where you see relationships among the various items. On each connecting line, write a word or phrase that states how the items are related.

5. At the top of this sheet, write "The Self Apart." Spend a few minutes reflecting on your drawing and record your responses to the following questions: What immediately grabs my attention? What feelings or emotions does this drawing evoke in me? What are the most interesting and informative patterns or connections? Which of these individualistic patterns and connections are strongest in my life? Which are weakest? What are the pluses and minuses of "The Self Apart"?

6. Set this drawing aside and proceed immediately to exercise 2.

Exercise 2: The Self as a Part

1. Play a piece of slow, meditative music, preferably a piece that has no immediately discernable melody or beat, such as something by Steven Halpern or Don Campbell, or sounds from nature. Draw a large circle on a sheet of large paper.

2. Close your eyes and visualize yourself standing with a group of people in a circle, holding hands. Concentrate on this group for a few minutes and see if you recognize any of the people. Some may be acquaintances. Others may be from the past. Some may be fictional. Some may be unknown.

3. With your eyes still closed, imagine that you are standing in the center of the circle. See yourself in the circle and this circle of people in you. You are one with the circle. Spend several minutes contemplating this awareness.

4. Open your eyes and draw many stick figures around the circle on your paper so that you get the impression that the circle looks like it is made up of people. Staying in touch with what you have seen and felt when visualizing the circle of people, list at least ten things that express your interpersonal understanding and feelings, and that express how you are an intimate part of other people and they a part of you.

5. For each item you have written draw a visual image. Draw lines of connection between the various items where you intuit relationships.

6. At the top of this sheet, write "The Self as a Part." Spend a few minutes reflecting on your drawing and record your responses to the following questions: What immediatlely grabs my attention? What feelings or emotions does this drawing evoke? What are the most interesting and informative patterns or connections? Which of these interpersonal patterns and connections are strongest in my life? Which are weakest? What are the pluses and minuses of "The Self as a Part"? Move immediately to the third exercise.

Exercise 3: The Self Apart *and* the Self as a Part

1. Place the two drawings side by side on the table before you. Spend a few minutes reflecting on the similarities and differences between the two drawings.

2. Focus on the first drawing for ten seconds (count the seconds in your head). Shift your attention to the second drawing for ten seconds. Shift back to the first drawing and concentrate on it for nine seconds. Shift your concentration to the second drawing for nine seconds. Continue shifting back and forth between the drawings, giving your full attention to each drawing for eight, seven, six, five, four, three, two seconds, then one second.

3. Play a piece of baroque music (try Pachelbel's Canon in D). Lie on the floor, close your eyes, and take several deep breaths to help you relax.

4. Imagine a blending of the two drawings taking place within you. Know and experience yourself as an individual, as a self apart. Let the full potential of that individualistic self flow into you and sense how it can empower your relationships with other people. Know and experience yourself as an intimate part of other people, as the self as a part. Let the full potential of that interpersonal self flow into you and sense how it can empower your being as an individual. Allow at least five minutes for this blending to occur.

5. When you feel this blending has occurred, open your eyes, take a third sheet of flip chart paper, and create a drawing or symbolic representation that in some way expresses the "Blended Self." Spend a few minutes recording your reflections, feelings, insights, and discoveries as you did these three exercises.

Intrapersonal Intelligence

Watching the Mind

I Think; Therefore I Am . . . Intelligent!

> *To help you develop mindfulness—or mind-fullness (as opposed to mind-lessness)—this practice asks you to step back and watch yourself doing a variety of ordinary activities.*

Phase 1: Developing Mindfulness

Getting Started

For this exercise, you will need several fifteen- to twenty-minute blocks of time, preferably on different days. You'll need a space where you can be alone and uninterrupted.

Basic Process

In this practice you will learn how to pay attention to the often missed details of many routine parts of daily living. The exercise outlines the basic procedures.

Exercise: The Basic Mindfulness Process

Following are some basic steps for practicing mindfulness. You can apply these steps to almost any task. Following the description of the basic practice are some suggestions for adapting the practice to a variety of ordinary activities.

1. Perform a routine task in slow motion so you can watch each part of the task as you perform it.

2. Keep your full attention on the task itself. Do not worry about when it will be over or what you will do after you have finished. Simply watch yourself carefully.

3. When extraneous thoughts or feelings arise, note them, but do not become caught up in them. Let them pass of their own accord, like bubbles floating on the wind. Return to your mindful observation of the task you are performing.

4. When you have completed the task, reflect on it by answering the following questions: What did you notice? What are your observations? What discoveries did you make? What are your feelings about the exercise? What was surprising? Most interesting? What did you learn about yourself and how your mind operates?

Following are some possible situations in which you might try the mindfulness practice. Use the process outlined above with each suggestion: Eat a single raisin or a grape in a very mindful fashion. Choose a room in your home around whose perimeter you can walk; walk in very slow motion, paying attention to everything that goes on in the walking process. Practice brushing your teeth, washing the dishes, or folding the laundry. After performing a task that requires a great deal of physical energy (tennis, aerobic exercise, and so on) practice being aware of its total effect on you.

After several weeks of doing this exercise, reflect on what has happened to you and your awareness by answering the following questions: What do you remember? What experiences stand out in your mind? What are your feelings? What did you like? What was surprising? What was interesting? What was most difficult? What did you learn about yourself and your inner processes? How do you need or want to use this exercise in the future?

Phase 2: Clearing and Stilling the Mind

Getting Started

To experience the full benefits of this exercise, you will need to set aside a minimum of fifteen minutes a day for at least two weeks. Choose a quiet and uncluttered space for the practice, a space where you can be alone and will not be interrupted. Do the practice at the same time and in the same place each day.

Basic Process

This exercise introduces you to the basic process of clearing and stilling the mind.

Exercise 1: Clearing and Stilling the Mind*

Following are some basic steps for clearing and stilling the mind. Following the description of the process are six techniques that may help you maintain your active awareness during the practice sessions.

1. Sit in a relaxed yet attentive position with your feet flat on the floor. Straighten your spine and head so that your breathing is free and easy. Fold your hands in

*Adapted from Lazear, David. 1991. *Seven Ways of Knowing: Teaching for Multiple Intelligences* (Palatine, Ill.: Skylight).

your lap or rest them palms down on your thighs. Keep your eyes open but slightly downcast. Stare at a blank wall or a table top that is free of distracting objects. Establish an awake, alert posture.

2. Focus your attention on your breathing. Breathe deeply from the lower abdomen, allowing your stomach to expand and contract naturally, as if you were blowing up a beach ball. Just relax and focus on this process. Your breathing will probably become deeper and slower as you focus on it.

3. Allow the mind to be free, open, and unattached. As thoughts and sensations arise, simply observe them. Let them come and go naturally. Do not get caught up in them. When the mind wanders, as it will, gently but firmly bring it back to the task of focusing on your posture, your breath, and the process of the mind itself.

Sit for at least fifteen minutes, maintaining an active awareness of yourself just sitting. Don't think or analyze what you're doing. Don't evaluate yourself. *Just sit and watch and be still.* Try each of the following techniques during different practice sessions and see which one works best.

> **Intensifying awareness of NOWNESS:** Let go of any concerns and thoughts that are on your mind; bring your full awareness to the present moment, to right now. For now your task is to experience yourself, detached from these things.
>
> **Counting your breaths:** Inhale deeply and on the exhalation count to yourself "one." Inhale again and on the exhalation count "two." Continue to ten. Then try for fifteen, twenty, and so on, without losing track of the process of breathing. If you get distracted and lose track of the counting, start again with one.
>
> **Dealing with the wandering mind:** Imagine that the thoughts are mere bubbles floating on the wind. Simply watch them until they naturally disappear or float away, and don't let yourself get caught up in the thoughts. Gently but firmly bring yourself back to the task of being aware of your sitting and breathing.
>
> **Dealing with outside distractions:** When something grabs your attention, note the distraction, but treat it as having no more consequence than vanishing steam from a boiling pot. Acknowledge it and immediately return your attention to the task of watching the process of your breathing and your sitting.
>
> **Labeling mind processes:** When you notice that you have started brooding on some thought or concern, step back from it. Note the mental process, then return to watching the breath and your sitting.
>
> **Stopping the mind:** As soon as you are aware that your mind has started thinking about something, cut the thought off. Immediately refocus your attention on your breathing. Catch the mind starting to think about something almost before it begins, then stop the thought.

After two weeks of doing this exercise every day, reflect on what has happened to you and your awareness by answering the following questions: What do you remember? What experiences stand out in your mind? What are your feelings? What did you like? What was surprising? What was interesting? What was most difficult? What did you learn about yourself and your inner processes? How do you need and want to use this exercise in the future? In what everyday situations can you use this exercise?

Phase 3: Concentrating the Mind

Getting Started

You will need to set aside a minimum of fifteen minutes a day for at least two weeks. Choose a quiet and uncluttered space where you can be alone and uninterrupted. Do the practice at the same time and in the same place each day.

Basic Process

The first exercise introduces you to the basic process of concentrating the mind, and exercise 2 suggests ways to extend the basic process into everyday life.

Exercise 1: The Basic Concentration Process

Following are some basic steps for focusing the mind. Following the description of the process are several techniques that may help you maintain your focused awareness during the different practice sessions.

1. Select one concentration object from the following list.

2. Sit in a relaxed yet attentive position, close your eyes, and take several deep breaths, breathing from your abdomen. Relax as completely as you can, thinking of nothing but inhalation and exhalation.

3. With each exhalation allow yourself to relax more, letting go of any thoughts or concerns.

4. Open your eyes and perform the exercise that is described for the concentration object you have chosen. See how long you can remain focused on the object without other thoughts coming into your mind. Don't analyze or think about the object; just experience it, keeping the mind clear and open.

5. When something distracts you, simply acknowledge the distraction, close your eyes, take several deep breaths, then open your eyes and return your concentration to the object.

Start with the first object and work with it until you feel some degree of mastery, then move to the next one. Try a different one during each practice session for two weeks, and see which one works best for you.

> Ring a bell, and focus on the sound. See how long you can continue to hear the ringing. When you can no longer hear it, ring the bell again; extend your experience of hearing the ring.

Place a piece of hard candy in your mouth and suck on it for about thirty seconds, then remove the candy. Focus on the experience of its taste. When you can no longer experience the taste, suck on it again for another thirty seconds; extend your experience of the taste.

Inhale deeply several times a bottle of cologne, a fragrant flower, a can of nuts, or a burning stick of incense. Move the object away from you and see how long you can continue to smell it. When you can no longer sense the fragrance, smell it again; extend your experience of it.

Place a lighted candle before you. Focus on the flame. Don't analyze it or think about it. Just gaze at the flame and allow it to mesmerize you. Become one with the flame!

Choose an object from nature, such as a pinecone, a flower, a shell, or a rock. Focus on the object. Don't analyze it or think about it. Just experience it totally.

Choose a picture that contains a circular pattern. Focus on the pattern, ignoring everything else in the picture. Squint your eyes to blur the rest of the picture. Don't analyze or think about the pattern. Just experience it.

Select a piece of new age music or select a tape or CD of environmental sounds. Play the music and focus on the sound. Don't analyze the music, the sounds, or their impact on you. Just experience the auditory stimuli.

After two weeks reflect on this exercise by answering the following questions: What do you remember? What experiences stand out in your mind? What are your feelings? What did you like? What was surprising? What was interesting? What was most difficult? What did you learn about your inner processes? How will you use this exercise?

Exercise 2: Concentrating the Mind in Everyday Life

Think about everyday situations in which it is important to be able to focus the mind for a period of time without being distracted by the myriad activities going on around you. Use your ability to concentrate in situations such as the following:

1. Preparing a report, paper, or speech on short notice, in a less than ideal setting you need to *focus on the task at hand and ignore feelings about the task or distractions.*

2. Reading something you need to understand while in a distracting environment you need to *focus fully on the words and screen out distractions.*

The Inner Advisory Council

Here's My Problem— What's Your Advice?

Figuratively speaking, we all have a host of people who live inside our heads—various heroes, relatives, friends, even enemies. Some of these figures are fictional and others are real. Some may be human beings while others may be animals or mythological creatures.

Phase 1: Who Is Sitting on My Inner Council?

Getting Started

You will need an hour or so of uninterrupted time for this exercise and a space in which you feel relaxed and that is conducive to serious thinking. You'll also need several sheets of blank paper and five large index cards.

Basic Process

The following exercise invites you to get to know your inner council. You will mentally convene the council, discuss a problem, and explore the possibilities for using the council's advice.

1. Brainstorm a list of at least ten issues, concerns, challenges, or problems with which you are currently struggling.

2. Using a chart with the headings *Historical Figures, Characters from Fiction, Figures in the News,* and *Personal Figures,* brainstorm at least five favorite characters for each category.

3. Select one item from your issues list and one character per column from the chart, a person with whom you wish you could sit down and discuss your concern.

4. Write each character's name on a separate index card and prop the cards up in front of you. Pretend that you and these four characters are sitting together in your living room. Create the script of this dialogue, writing what you imagine each person would say in such a conversation.

5. Continue the script on another sheet of paper, pretending you are responding to their advice. Write your responses to, questions about, and arguments with the advice given in the preceding conversation. Then imagine what each advisor would say in response to your responses, questions, and arguments. Also write what you imagine they might say in response to one another.

6. When you feel that you have enough advice, stop and read the script. Reflect on what you have written using the following questions: What parts stand out in your mind? What advice was totally expected, boring, or the "same old, same old"? What advice do you find most appealing and why? What advice do you find most interesting and why? What forced you to think about something you hadn't considered before? With which pieces of advice do you flatly disagree and why? With what pieces of advice do you totally agree and why? Which pieces of advice do you need to ponder further and what do you need to think about in your ponderings?

Phase 2: Whom Do I Need on My Inner Council?

Getting Started

You will need an hour or so of uninterrupted time for this exercise, and a space in which you feel relaxed and that is conducive to serious thinking. You will also need several sheets of blank paper and at least ten large index cards.

Basic Process

In the first exercise you'll have a chance to talk with characters who have perspectives that may be very different from your own. The second exercise will lead you into higher-order thinking and creativity as you enter into dialogues with unusual persons and things.

Exercise 1: Expanding and Diversifying the Inner Council

1. Using a chart with the headings, *People whose religious or spiritual persuasions differ from mine, People of the opposite sex, People whose political perspectives differ from mine, People whose socioeconomic situations differ from mine, People whose sexual orientation differs from mine, People in cultures other than my own, Contemporary figures whose lifestyles and perspectives differ from mine,* and *People who almost always disagree with me no matter what the topic,* brainstorm at least three people or characters for each category.

   Having a dialogue with these people can help to deepen your understanding of your own values and beliefs. They may reveal your blind spots, prejudices, and unthought-through assumptions.

2. Select a different item from the one you chose in the previous exercise.

3. Select ten characters to sit on your inner council. Use people from the previous exercise as well as from the list you just created, with at least five coming from the chart you just created.

4. Write the names of these ten people on ten separate index cards and arrange them in a circle on the floor, as if you were sitting in the circle with them. Pretend that you and these people are discussing your concern. Record at least one response per person of what you imagine each person would contribute to the discussion.

5. Continue the script on another sheet of paper, writing your responses to, questions about, and arguments with the advice given and what you imagine the people would say in response to you as well as to one another.

6. When you feel that you've had enough advice, stop and read over the script. Reflect on what you have written using the questions you used in the previous exercise.

Exercise 2: Extraordinary Members of the Inner Council

Using the same basic process that you used in the previous two exercises, experiment with any of the following dialogue scenarios. Have lots of fun and be creative. **Note:** Don't dismiss any of these scenarios as too weird. Each dialogue has the possibility of opening undiscovered aspects of yourself and tapping your creative problem-solving potentials.

Scenarios

Make a list of descendants, friends, political figures, entertainers, and so on that you may meet in the future.

Make a list of some of your organs or systems.

Make a list of natural objects or events (a mountain, a thunderstorm, and so on).

Make a list of religious and cultural symbols that are part of your life.

Make a list of pets, animals that you like or dislike, animals in stories, mythological creatures, and so on.

Make a list of inanimate objects that are a regular part of your daily life (computer, car, VCR, refrigerator, and so on).

Make a list of movie characters who have made an impression on you.

Make a list of physical senses (taste, touch, and so on) as well as non-physical senses (intuitive sense, religious sensibility, and so on).

Tapping Your Latent Potentials

Be All That You Can Be!

> *This practice will help you get in touch with your capacities for inspiration and renewal and your subtle, perhaps unconscious, creative problem-solving abilities.*

Tapping Untapped Abilities

Getting Started

Begin with the scenarios that you find most intriguing or that look enjoyable. Give yourself plenty of uninterrupted time and try each scenario several times. Part of what you are doing is seeding your creativity, which can't be rushed.

Basic Process

The practice explores issues and challenges in your life through a variety of imagination scenarios. These scenarios will access various aspects of your inner wisdom and creativity, which you may not have tapped fully before, to help you deal with your concerns.

1. Using a chart with the headings, *Issues/Concerns, Challenges I Face, Goals I'm Pursuing, Problems I Face,* and *Things That Worry Me,* brainstorm at least five issues for each column.

2. Select one item from each column and choose at least one of the following imagination scenarios for exploring answers to it. Give yourself several days to work with the scenarios you have chosen. Note similarities and differences in the information you receive when you repeat the scenario.

3. After each imagination scenario, reflect on your experience by answering these questions: What was the basic information or advice you received? What information or advice was expected or predictable? What was a surprise? What information helped give you a new way to think about your concern? How was it helpful? How has the issue shifted? Next time you use this scenario, what new aspects of your concern do you want or need to explore? What changes do you want to make? What have you learned about tapping your creative potentials?

The Imagination Scenarios

Imagine that you have an inner coach who knows you intimately. She will help you develop any skill that you want to develop.

Pretend that you have access to an unlimited number of self-help TV shows. Every show is focused on giving you insight to issues in your life.

Imagine that you have a special time machine that can instantly transport you into the future.

Think about an upcoming event or situation and imagine yourself giving an exemplary performance.

Imagine that your brain is an interactive video game with a wide selection of creative thinking software.

Think of a person from the past, real or fictional, with whom you intimately identify. Imagine that this person is your closest friend who knows you, who cares about you and your welfare more than anyone else you know.

Think of a skill you want to learn or improve, and of a master of that skill. Imagine that you are this person's shadow.

Metacognition

Thinking about Thinking

> *Do you talk to yourself? Do you answer yourself? What do you talk to yourself about? Why do you engage in this activity? You might be interested to know that you are exhibiting metacognitive behavior.*
>
> *This practice is about learning to have increasingly fruitful conversations with yourself.*

Phase 1: Higher-Order Thinking and Creativity

Getting Started

This exercise requires a partner. Choose someone you trust.

Basic Process

In this exercise, you and your partner practice several levels of thinking.

Exercise 1: Higher-Order Thinking

1. With your partner, study the following descriptions of three levels of thinking.

    ◆ **Objective thinking ("Just the facts, ma'am, nothing but the facts")** To prompt this level of thinking, start a sentence with one of the following or perform the given task:

How many	*Describe*	*Match*
Recite	*Select*	*List*
Count	*Recall*	*Name*
Pick out	*Calculate*	*Repeat*
Summarize	*Identify*	*Define*

    ◆ **Process thinking ("How did you solve that problem? What process did you use?")** To prompt this level of thinking, start a sentence with one of the following or perform the given task:

Compare and contrast	*Divide into parts*	*Solve*
Explain why	*Classify*	*Analyze*
Distinguish	*Reason*	*Decipher*
Argue	*Discern*	*Teach*
Rank	*Demonstrate*	*Prove*

    ◆ **Application thinking ("How can I use it in my everyday life?")** To prompt this level of thinking, start a sentence with one of the following or perform the given task:

Evaluate	*Apply*	*Judge*
Determine	*If/then*	*Estimate*
Apply a principle	*Forecast*	*Conclude*
Synthesize	*Hypothesize*	*Predict*
Imagine	*Weigh up*	*Suppose*

2. Together, choose an article or editorial from the newspaper, a well-known story, a famous quotation or saying, words from a popular song, a TV show or movie you have both recently seen, a favorite poem, or a conversation with another person in which you were both involved.

3. Individually select three words from each "starter list" and write three discussion questions per level for the item.

4. When you have each completed your questions, exchange them and write answers to each other's questions.

5. Share your answers with each other and reflect on the kinds of thinking your questions provoked. What obvious differences in the thinking or answers do you notice between the different levels? Which level of questions did you enjoy the most? Which were boring? Which were most difficult? Which were most creative or produced new or surprising thoughts? Did your questions provoke the level of thinking you were intending? Together rewrite or refine any questions you think could be better.

6. Brainstorm ways you could use this process in your daily lives (include ideas for your personal and professional lives).

Who Am I, Really?

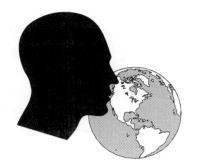

What's It All About, Alfie?

> *Throughout the ages, many people have prodded humanity to think about the meaning of life. Consider the intrapersonal proddings of Jesus, Gautama the Buddha, Socrates, Joan of Arc, Mohammed, and others.*

Phase 1: What Really Matters?*

Getting Started

You will need an empty can, matches, and thirty slips of 3-by-5-inch paper. You will probably need about one hour of uninterrupted time for the exercise.

Basic Process

This practice helps you evaluate what is really important to you. Imagining that you have only the bare essentials, you reflect on what really matters.

Brainstorming What's Important

In a chart with the headings, *Possessions, Relationships with People or Pets, Skills I Have, Beliefs and Values,* and *Personal Symbols,* list at least five items under each heading that are currently important in your life. When you have completed the chart, write each item on a separate slip of paper.

The Game Process

Following are the basic procedures. Feel free to add your own embellishments. Don't cop out! If you don't like this version of the game, *do* create your own version to work on the important intrapersonal issues that the game investigates.

1. Imagine that you are going on a long journey that will take many years and that will take you to a country that is very different from your own. From the slips of paper, select those items that you will have to leave behind as you start the journey. Tear up these slips of paper and toss them into the can.

2. Your guide informs you that, due to new regulations in this country, each person must discard five items before proceeding. From your remaining slips of paper, select five items. Tear up these slips of paper and toss them into the can.

*Adapted from Lazear, David. 1991. *Seven Ways of Knowing: Teaching for Multiple Intelligences* (Palatine, Ill.: Skylight).

3. Due to a terrible mistake, the expedition has gone bankrupt. To continue and survive you must get a job in a field that you know nothing about. In fact some of the abilities that made you successful in the past are now a hindrance. From the slips of paper, select those items that you must give up. Again, tear them into pieces and toss them into the can.

4. Things have deteriorated so much that your very self-identity is preventing the success of the journey and is threatening your well-being. You therefore decide to become a new person. Once again, select the slips of paper that contain items that have to go. Tear these up and toss them into the can.

5. Take the can outside and drop a lighted match into it. Contemplate the items that are going up in smoke.

6. Write a short essay entitled "The Real Me" or "Who Am I?" based on your experience of and responses to the game.

Reflect on the exercise using the following question: What are your general observations about the game? What stands out? What did you find most interesting? What was surprising? What was disturbing? What real-life situations does this game remind you of? When have you experienced having to give up things that are important to you? What have you learned about yourself? If you were to tell someone else what this game is about in one sentence, what would you say? When do you want to play this game again? What alterations and adaptations do you want to make?

Phase 2: My Future Life

Getting Started

You will probably want to stretch this practice over several days, for new thoughts will likely occur after you get started. It is not intended to be completed in a single sitting.

Basic Process

You begin by anticipating people, places, and events you may encounter in your future. You create a time line that gives you a picture of the future as you see it today and use the time line for reflection.

1. Begin by listing as many items as you can on a chart with the headings, *People I Anticipate Will Be Part of My Future, Things I Want to Accomplish before My Death, Experiences I Will Have in the Future, Places I Want to Live or Visit,* and *Other Things That Will Probably Be Part of My Future.* Have fun! Be wild! Don't rule out anything that occurs to you.

2. Choose a year well into your future. Subtract the current year. Get a time line from your teacher. Divide this number by five, then divide the section of the time line labeled "year" into this many segments. Number each segment with a five-year span starting with the current year (for example, 1996–2001, 2001–2006).

 ◆ Look at the lists on the chart. Plot each item on the time line in the five-year segment you think it might occur. Allow yourself to be intuitive and have fun.

 ◆ Look over the events and see if you can divide your future into three to five potential stages. Don't worry about being too precise. When you sense a stage, draw a line through the "years" row to the bottom of the time line.

 ◆ Make up a brief, descriptive title for each stage and write these titles in the appropriate spaces above the years row.

 ◆ Look for themes that seem to run through these stages. On the top row write a title for your future.

3. When you have completed the time line, read it over and ask yourself the following questions: What immediately catches your attention? Which stage do you find most surprising? What about that stage surprises you? Which looks most interesting? Which do you anticipate will be the most exciting? Why? What major changes do you sense are somehow part of your future? In what ways does your life today influence your future direction? What changes do you need to make to ensure that certain things happen? What changes do you need to make to prevent certain things from happening?

4. Store your time line in a convenient place. Every three months or so, review it, answering the questions listed above. Get out your calendar and mark a date right now to remind you to revisit the future when the date rolls around.

Reflective Journals*

What Am I Thinking, Feeling, and Sensing?

> *The capacity for self-reflection adds an important dimension to our living that, as far as we know, is unique to humans.*

Setting Up Your Reflective Journal

Getting Started

Set up a loose-leaf notebook with five dividers labeled "Daily Log," "Weekly Log," "Turning Points," "Future Discourses," and "Other Logs." After each divider include at least five blank pages for entries.

*Adapted from Lazear, David. 1991. *Seven Ways of Knowing: Teaching for Multiple Intelligences* (Palatine, Ill.: Skylight).

Basic Process

You will need to start a daily and weekly reflection on your life. I have provided suggestions for journal entries, but feel free to improvise. You are also invited to keep a journal about other dimensions of your life—turning points from the past and various aspects of your future.

1. At the end of each day write down three things that happened that you want to remember, three things you've been thinking about, and three difficult things about the day. Give the day a title.

2. On Saturday or Sunday reflect on the past week. Turn your journal sideways and write the days of the week across the top. Look over your daily logs for this week and record the most important items from each day in the appropriate column. Divide your chart into two parts. For each part, make up a title that in some way communicates what this week was like for you. Then create a title for the whole week at the top of the chart.

3. Look back over any segment of your life that you want to understand in terms of its impact. Brainstorm a list of key events from this period that have in some way shaped who you are today (for example, a book you read that changed your thinking, the death of a friend, a memorable trip). Arrange the events in chronological order, then write several sentences expressing how each event has shaped you and who you understand yourself to be.

4. Brainstorm a list of events you anticipate will be part of your future. For each item, imagine that the event is doing the writing in your journal. What would it record in your journal for today? Following are some possible future events to get you started: the coming year, the next decade, the birth of your great-grandchildren, a trip to a place you want to visit, an experience you want to have, an outing with a future pet, an exercise session, your retirement years, an event of a club or organization, a family reunion 25 years from now.

Don't try to do this activity in one sitting. Get started, then let it happen and grow naturally as your journaling becomes more interesting to you. Create your own list of possible events. Choose aspects of your future to dialogue with that would benefit you

Your Life as an Epic Journey

"Once upon a Time . . . "

> *This practice deals with archetypal figures; an archetypal figure embodies life struggles, profound knowings, deep emotions, and qualities that are universal to humanity. Learning to identify our seemingly petty concerns and struggles with universal archetypes can ennoble and deepen our experience.*

Phase 1: Understanding My Life Journey through the Journey of Another

Getting Started

You will probably need to allow several hours, spread over several days, for this exercise. It may take you deeper than you thought it would at first glance. Whatever happens, don't rush the process; let it unfold naturally.

Basic Process

The exercise first asks you to think about figures who are, for whatever reason, important to you. You will then parallel your life journey with theirs, reflecting on what you can learn and have already learned from them.

1. Brainstorm a list of at least ten historical or fictional characters with whom you feel a deep connection.

2. Choose a character from your list and divide his or her life into five stages. Use a chart with headings across the top and down the left column to analyze your character's journey. The headings along the top are *Stage 1, Stage 2,* etc. The left column headings are *Events That Occurred in This Stage, Character's Feelings in This Stage, Character's Discoveries in This Stage, Character's Learnings from This Stage,* and *My Title for This Stage of the Character's Journey.*

3. Reflect on your own life journey in and through the journey of this character. For each stage of the journey, record your responses to the following questions: When did I experience similar events? When did I experience similar feelings? When did I make similar discoveries? What learnings parallel my own life learnings?

4. Reflect on this exercise by asking yourself the following questions: What parallels are most striking? What do I find most interesting? Most surprising or unexpected? Most disturbing? What have I learned about my own life? What new questions about my life have been raised?

Phase 2: Retelling My Life Journey as a Myth

Getting Started

It will probably seem a bit strange at first to think that your life could be an example for others. However, doing so can lead to profound levels of your own being of which you have not been aware. Again, allow plenty of time, and let it unfold naturally.

Basic Process

You will reflect on important events, then write a myth or epic in which you are the hero who is journeying where no human being has gone before.

1. Make a list of at least fifteen significant events that have happened in your life. On your list include such things as important decisions you made, unexpected fortune that came your way, major accomplishments, and disasters. When you have completed your list, rewrite it in chronological order.

2. Look at the list to see which events were turning points in your life. Use a chart with the headings *Stage 1, Stage 2*, etc. and the following down the left side: *Things That Happened to Me in This Stage, My Feelings during This Stage, My Discoveries during This Stage, My Learnings from This Stage*, and *My Title for This Stage of My Journey*.

3. Your life journey is a journey that can help others. Imagine yourself as a mythological figure and the various stages of your journey as archetypal stages with which others can identify and find guidance for their journeys. Take five pages of blank paper, staple them together, and on the first page, using colored pens, write "The Fantastic Journey of (your name)."

   On the second page write "𝕺nce upon a time, . . . " then just keep writing, telling your life story in mythic terms: you are the hero, and the various events you experienced are challenges you faced, battles you fought, monsters you defeated, people you rescued, and so on along the way. Be very creative with the facts. Remember, you're creating a myth that is symbolic. You want the reader of this tale to be drawn into it and to recognize his or her journey through yours.

   Don't try to complete the story in one sitting. Let it grow naturally over the course of several weeks. As new ideas occur to you, feel free to revise and rewrite whole sections of the story. In any event, try to fill all four pages with the story.

4. Select several people who are close to you to review your story. **DO NOT** tell them that it is a mythological retelling of your own life's journey. After they have read it, ask them what they remember from the story. What grabbed their attention?

5. Reflect on the process of looking at another's life journey, then creating your own as a myth. What did you learn? If you do it again, how will you do it differently?

Logical-Mathematical Intelligence

Logical Thought Patterns

*Say What You Mean;
Mean What You Say*

> *On any given day we employ a wide variety of thinking strategies and processes. Consider the different modes of thinking that are involved when you are deciding what to have for lunch, or counseling a family member about a personal problem.*

Phase 1: Understanding Cognitive Patterns

Getting Started

The exercises were designed for you to do on your own. However, you may find them more interesting and enjoyable with a partner or group.

Basic Process

Exercise 1 introduces you to a variety of cognitive organizers or maps. These organizers are visual designs of logical thinking processes. Exercise 2 asks you to analyze a story using the organizers.

Exercise 1: Using Cognitive Organizers

1. Following are ten cognitive organizers, each using a visual representation of a logical thinking pattern. Study each organizer and try the practice scenario (or better yet, make up one of your own).

Venn Diagram
Compare and Contrast Thinking

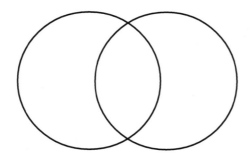

Basic Process: In each circle list characteristics that are unique to each item you are comparing and contrasting. In the overlapping area list attributes that the two have in common.

Practice Scenario: Compare/contrast your life now with your life one year ago.

Web
Brainstorm Thinking

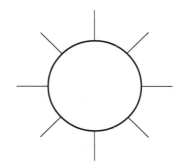

Basic Process: In the circle write the topic or concern that is your brainstorm focus. On the rays write all ideas that occur to you. Don't screen out anything; the only rule is that there must be some connection to the central topic.

Practice Scenario: Brainstorm attributes of your favorite music.

Ranking Ladder
Rank Order/Priority Thinking

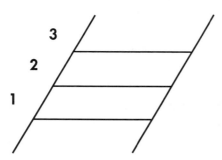

Basic Process: Take a list of items and put them in logical or priority order. Place the first item in the sequence on rung one of the ladder, then proceed to place each item on the appropriate rung.

Practice Scenario: Prioritize your work skills in terms of those that are most important or strongest.

Matrix
Classification Thinking

Side Category \ Top Category			

Basic Process: Along the top row list specific items to classify. In the first column list the criterion for each item on the top row. (The top left box will be blank.) In the boxes under each top item apply the criterion.

Practice Scenario: Classify/analyze members of your family (top row) in terms of personality traits (first column criteria).

The 5 Ws
Inferential/Inductive Thinking

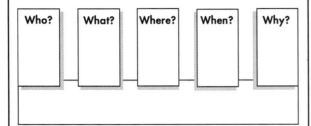

Basic Process: In the five boxes on top, list the particulars of the situation being analyzed—*who, what, when, where,* and *why.* In the second row make general statements about the situation. (In other words, use the particulars to draw conclusions.)

Practice Scenario: Take an article from the newspaper or a magazine and apply the 5 Ws model to it, or analyze a difficult situation at work.

Thought Tree
Generalized/Deductive Thinking

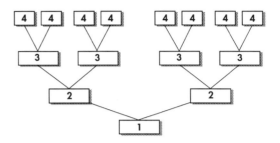

Basic Process: In the bottom box write a word, a hobby, a name, or some other topic. In the row above it, write two things you associate with the item. In the next row up, make associations with the previous two associations. In the fourth row make associations with the previous associations.

Practice Scenario: In the first box write the name of your favorite food, then move up, making associations and further associations.

PMI Chart
Thinking about Opposite Points of View

P+	M–	I?

Basic Process: Choose a topic, then a point of view different from your own. In the first column write positive aspects of this viewpoint. In the second column write negative aspects. In the third column write what's interesting about this point of view.

Practice Scenario: Use the PMI chart to consider a religious belief that is different from your own.

Concept Map
Nonlinear Relationship Thinking

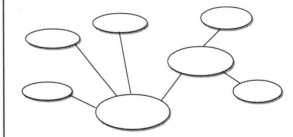

Basic Process: In the central circle write the concept or topic you want to explore. In the surrounding circles write the main aspects, dimensions, or perspectives associated with the central topic. Then web each of these aspects or associations.

Practice Scenario: Map one of your cherished values or a current sociopolitical issue.

Time Line **Sequential Thinking**	The Rating Scale **Comparing Against a Standard**
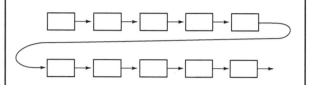	

Time Line
Sequential Thinking

Basic Process: Begin with a random list of items related to a specific topic, such as planning a party, parts of a story, a recipe, and so on. Arrange the list of items in the boxes, writing what comes first in the first box, what comes second in the second, and so on.

Practice Scenario: Brainstorm a "to do" list for the coming month and put it on a time line.

The Rating Scale
Comparing Against a Standard

Basic Process: List items you want to rate: your work skills, personality traits you want to develop, and so on. Then rate each item, writing it in the appropriate place on the 1-to-10 scale. Check the appropriate part of the scale (8–10 = WOW!, 4–7 = AVERAGE, and 0–3 = LOW.) **Note:** You decide the specific ranking standards.

Practice Scenario: Rate your people skills in a group situation (for example, listening, giving feedback, remembering names).

2. Reflect on your experience:

   ◆ Which of the organizers made the greatest impression?

   ◆ Which did you find most interesting? Which was most fun? Which was most difficult? Which did you like the most? Which did you dislike?

   ◆ Which of the organizers surprised you because of the thinking it helped you do? Which sparked the most creative thinking?

   ◆ What did you learn about yourself and your logical thinking patterns?

Exercise 2: Using Cognitive Organizers as Analytic Tools

1. Experiment with the cognitive organizers by applying them to a favorite story. Find a way to use each one of the cognitive organizers. Continue with your own adaptations of the cognitive organizer models. Have fun! Be creative!

2. Reflect on this exercise by answering the following questions: What immediately grabs your attention? Which organizer did you find most surprising? Which was most challenging? Which helped you come up with the most creative or insightful thinking? What did you learn about yourself? Was there one organizer through which you learned more than through the others? What other applications can you see for these cognitive maps?

Phase 2: Strategic Use of Cognitive Patterns

Getting Started

Complete phase 1. Do the exercise on your own, and don't rush the process. Give yourself plenty of time to complete it.

Basic Process

The purpose of this exercise is to help you find connections among and applications of the logical thinking patterns you worked with in phase 1. You adapt the cognitive maps to particular situations you face in your everyday life, then evaluate the results.

A Cognitive Strategic Planning Process

1. For each of the cognitive organizers, list several situations, issues, or concerns in your life where you could apply this thinking pattern.

2. Choose five situations, issues, or concerns from your lists and plan specific adaptations of the cognitive patterns to fit your situation.

3. Try the plans and evaluate the results. What general observations have you made? What especially strikes you about the thinking it provoked and the ideas it helped you generate? What do you find most surprising about this experiment? What is most interesting?

4. Briefly evaluate the specific information you came up with using the organizers: What really seems on target, and what is off the wall? What information did you come up with that is beyond what you would have normally thought of? What information can you use (although not necessarily in its current form)?

5. Finally, evaluate the adaptations or "thinking tactics" you employed: What did you learn about applying this particular organizer to this kind of situation? If you apply this organizer to a similar situation, what will you do differently? What will you do the same? What other cognitive organizers might help you with this type of situation?

Problem Solving

What Would You Do If . . . ?

Improving Problem-Solving Skills

Getting Started

Give yourself a couple of weeks to work on these exercises. Get started and go as far as you want to, but plan to return to them often. Each time you return, look over your previous work. The incubation period between times may produce ideas that cause you to alter some of your earlier answers.

Basic Process

The first exercise asks you to become aware of your basic problem-solving technique, which underlies all of your conscious or unconscious problem solving. The second gives you an opportunity to evaluate each step of your problem-solving process. The third exercise invites you to look at an effective problem-solving model and to brainstorm strategies you could add to your current process.

Exercise 1: Becoming Aware of Your Problem-Solving Process

1. Brainstorm ten recent problems or challenges you have faced in your life.

2. Choose three of these challenges and write down the step-by-step process you used to solve the problem. List the formal and informal steps of the process. A formal step might be listing the pros and cons of possible solutions; an informal step might be discussing the problem with a friend.

3. Look over the steps and note those strategies you used in all three situations, those you used in two, and those you used in only one. List these in a chart with appropriate headings.

4. Reflect on your lists and extrapolate what your normal problem-solving process is. List the steps.

Exercise 2: Evaluating Your Problem-Solving Process

1. Look over the problem-solving method you articulated. Rank the steps of your current method: 1 = Works very well for me—provides me with the information I need; 2 = Not 100 percent effective—it gets me by; 3 = No way! Needs major help.

2. Analyze how you ranked the steps by answering the following questions: What characteristics of steps ranked 1 make them so effective? What do you like most about these steps? How do they serve you well? What characteristics of steps ranked 2 make them less effective? In what ways do they help you get by? What would need to change for these steps to become great? Elaborate on what's wrong with steps ranked 3. Why don't they work at all? If you were going to totally overhaul these steps, what changes would you make?

Exercise 3: Transforming Your Problem-Solving Process*

1. In the following model, the first two steps analyze all factors affecting the situation. Only after you have a thorough understanding of the situation, including your own hopes and dreams for it and frustrations about it, do you plan the action and implement it.

   Step 1. Latent Vision (*What's trying to be born?*) Read between the lines of your hopes and dreams; note things you would like to change. Imagine you are standing 2 to 3 months in the future when the problem is gone and then describe what it's like.

   Step 2. Underlying Challenges (*What's got to be figured out if the vision is to happen?*) If you don't know the underlying challenges, you can waste a lot of time and energy working on the wrong things.

*Adapted from a strategic planning process created by the Ecumenical Institute (EI) and Institute of Cultural Affairs (ICA).

Step 3. **Strategic Proposals** *(What must be done to meet the challenges?)* Discern the broad strategic pathways that will effectively deal with the challenges. Remember, the way to that future is through the challenges. Proposals are your major strategies for dealing with the challenges. Create a variety of fresh, bold, creative, and inspiring approaches.

Step 4. **Tactical Steps** *(What's it going to take to put wheels on the proposals?)* It's time to get on with it! Tactics are the nitty-gritty steps that must happen for you to actualize the directions.

Step 5. **Implementing Time Line** *(What, when, where, how, and who?)* This time line is the place of action, assignments, budgets, and calendars. Remember, as the implementation process begins, the challenges and blocks will change (if the tactics are on target). Thus, new and revised proposals and tactics will be required.

2. Go back to the articulation of your problem-solving process (step 4 of exercise 1). Compare this process with the one presented above and respond to the following questions: What are the similarities between the two models? Differences? What do you like about the new model? What do you not like? What is better in your model? What in the new model could improve your problem-solving method?

3. How would you redesign or modify your basic problem-solving process in light of the thinking you have been doing in this exercise?

Logical Thinking

Run That by Me Again. How Did You Get Here from There?

> *This practice deals with the type of thinking for which Spock has become an archetype—logical thinking to the extreme, or the logic side of logical-mathematical intelligence. You need these logic skills any time you are trying to convince others of a course of action or when you are involved in a discussion or debate on a controversial topic.*

Pushing Logic to the Limit

Getting Started

Work on each format, but plan to come back to each several times, because new ideas and thoughts will occur to you. Stay with each format until you have each of the boxes or triangles filled.

Basic Process

The two exercises that follow start with an example of how to use each format. You then choose a topic and build your own 4 x 4 x 4 and set of triangles.

Exercise 1: 4 x 4 x 4 Process

1. Following is an example of a basic 4 x 4 x 4. The format is designed to help you think logically through the possible points and perspectives for a presentation, an idea, an argument, and so on. This example is the beginning of a 4 x 4 x 4 on the topic "Healthy Living." (You can create your own blank form.)

1. Diet	Lower fat intake	skim milk	Balanced/ nutritious	grains	Cooking procedures	broiling	Eating practices	water intake
		sauces		veggies		steaming		eat slowly
		dressings		proteins		poaching		enjoy/savor
		snacks		dairy/fruit		roasting		stopping
2. Exercise	Cardio- vascular	jogging	Weight training	machines	Staying active	walking		
		Stairmaster		barbells		stairs		
		cycling		stretching		swimming		
		treadmill		dumbbells		sports		
3. Lifestyle	Personal habits	alcohol	Nonwork interests	hobbies				
		tobacco		friends				
		sexuality		movies				
		drugs		fun reading				
4. Stress	Relaxation procedures	meditation						
		breathing						
		massage						
		imagery						

2. Brainstorm a list of at least ten topics that you find especially interesting.

3. Select one item from your list and pretend that you must deliver a compelling presentation to an audience of four hundred people. Use the 4 x 4 x 4 format to plan your presentation. In the first column list the four main points of your speech. In the second, the four main supportive subpoints for main point 1. Continue listing subpoints for main points 2, 3, and 4. Then for each subpoint, list four subpoints. You can jump around the chart in a fairly random fashion, filling in ideas and examples as they come to you. Trust your intuitions and your first impressions. Have fun!

4. Reflect on this exercise by answering the following questions: What grabs your attention? Which part do you find most interesting? Most surprising? In what ways did the process help you? What did you like about it? What new discoveries did you make or new insights did you have? What discoveries did you make or insights did you have about yourself and your logical thought processes? List times when you can use the 4 x 4 x 4 process.

Exercise 2: Triangular Logic

1. Following are triangles within triangles within triangles. Working within this format can help you build your capacities for creating logical, internal consistency in a report, a presentation, or an essay, or when you simply want to challenge yourself to think through an issue thoroughly. Here is an example of triangular logic on the topic "The Social Process," which was developed by the Ecumenical Institute and Institute of Cultural Affairs. (You can create your own triangles.)

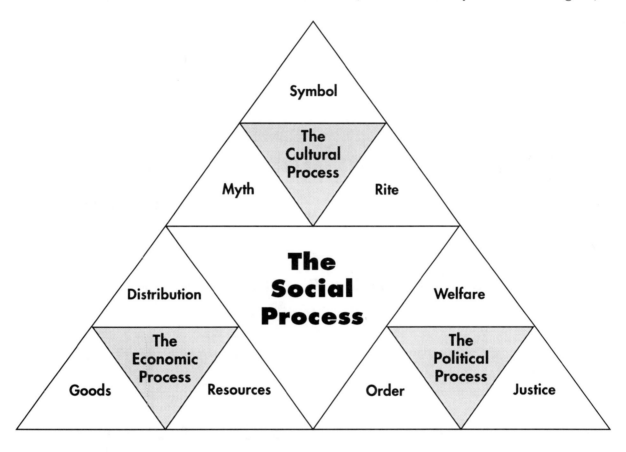

2. Choose another topic from the list of topics you brainstormed in step 2 of the previous exercise. Use the triangle format to help you think through the topic.

   ◆ Each lower left triangle contains items that are *foundational* or *sustaining* to the topic, that is, "the basics" or the "minimum requirements." For instance, you can see in the example that without the basic economic process (goods, resources, and production), there is no society. This triangle is the "that without which" aspect of the topic.

   ◆ Each lower right triangle contains the *organizational* aspects of the topic, that is, the "ordering" or "coordinating" dynamics. The example shows that once the basic requirements for sustaining a society are present, they must be orchestrated in some fashion.

   ◆ Each top triangle contains the *meaning-giving* or *values* dimension of the topic, that is, the "why this is important." For example, the cultural process invests the economic and political processes with myths, rituals, and symbols that communicate the values and beliefs of a people.

◆ Within each set of triangles, these main aspects are repeated. Thus, when you are working on the foundational pole, you should have a foundational/foundational triangle, a foundational/ordering triangle, and a foundational/meaning-giving triangle (and so on for the other two poles or sets of triangles).

3. Reflect on this exercise by responding to the following: What stands out? Which part of the triangles do you find most interesting? Most surprising? In what ways did the process help you? What did you like about it? What new discoveries did you make or new insights did you have about your topic? What discoveries did you make or insights did you have about yourself? List times when you could use the triangular process in your daily life.

Forcing Relationships

How are the president and a head of broccoli the same?

> *Creative thinking capacities are often at the heart of scientific breakthroughs.*

Exercising Nonlinear Thinking Processes

Getting Started

You may do these exercises with a group of friends. Once you have tried them with others, continue to work on them by yourself.

Basic Process

Start with the process of finding unusual, interesting, and unexpected relationships among ideas. Then you do a "forcing relationships analysis" of current issues. Finally you try forcing relationships as a way of forcing breakthroughs into the process of solving problems and meeting challenges.

Exercise 1: The Basic Process of Forcing Relationships

Play with the following sets of items and see what strange and interesting relationships your mind can discover. What do the items in column 1 have in common with the items in column 2? How many common areas can you find?

a snowflake
a hive of bees
an ice cream sundae
a rock song
the aroma of honeysuckle

a television
rush-hour traffic
a computer
your bank account
the governing body of your nation

Exercise 2: Forcing Relationships in Everyday Experiences

1. List five ordinary experiences you have had recently.

2. Divide each experience into five parts. Don't worry about things being in any sequence; just record all the pieces.

3. Create five new situations by combining items from different columns on the chart using the following pattern (follow each line to see which items to combine). For example, the third item in column 1 is now linked with the fourth item in column 2, the fifth in column 3, the fifth in column 4, and the fourth in column 5.

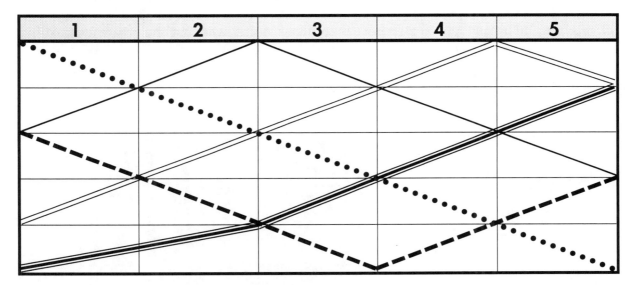

Write out the new scenario, filling in the details, so that it reads as a coherent experience.

Exercise 3: Forcing Relationships and the Daily News

1. Look at the chart on page 72 and imagine what the person in the first column might say to the audience in the second column about the topic in the third column.

2. To select scenarios, roll a die, count down that number in the first column, and circle that person. Roll for the second and third columns.

3. Imagine that you are the person addressing this particular audience on this chosen topic. Create an outline for a credible presentation.

The president of your country	A session of your national governing body	The current state of the nation
A famous rock star	A gathering of devoted rock fans	Promotion of a new album
A TV talk show host or personality	A typical talk show audience	The evening comedic monologue on the news
An evangelist	People gathered for a religious revival	Raising money for a special offering
A defense attorney	The jury in a criminal trial	Closing remarks defending a client's innocence in relation to the charges

Reflect on the exercises by responding to the following questions: What are your general observations? Which of the three exercises made the greatest impression on you? What did you find especially interesting? What was very unexpected? Which challenged you the most? Which were relatively easy? Which sparked the greatest creativity in your response? How would you explain the process to someone else? Why is this capacity important? What situations do you encounter every day that require you to force relationships? How could you adapt the processes to these situations?

Abstract Pattern Recognition

> *This practice deals with the ability to see concrete patterns and represent them in abstract, symbolic ways.*

The Subtle Patterns of Living

Getting Started

The first exercise will be more interesting with a group of friends, such as at a party. You need to perform exercises 2 and 3 alone, although you might ask interested friends to do the exercises too and then share the results.

Exercise 1: Guess the Pattern Games

1. Can you find the patterns in the following games? Find the pattern in each box, then try the games on your friends or colleagues. (Answers are found at the end of this practice.)

Which numbers come next in this sequence?

1, 2, 3, 6, 11, 20, 37, 68, 125, 230,

_____, _____, _____, _____

We are going on a journey. There are only certain items we can take with us. The following items are permissible:

apples, letters, margarine, zebras, bottles, kaleidoscopes, nuts, yarn, cotton, jazz, okra

What items may be included next?

_____   _____

_____   _____

_____   _____

_____   _____

Which symbols come next in this repeating pattern of symbols?

❋, Δ, ✓, #, •, ∞, +

+, ❋, Δ, ✓, #, •, ∞

∞, +, ❋, Δ, ✓, #, •

__, __, __

Word problems

A woman discovered that making and baking a pie took 80 minutes when she was wearing a wool jacket. However, when she did not wear the jacket, the same making and baking always took an hour and 20 minutes. Can you explain?

"I guarantee," said the clerk to Larry, "that this parrot will repeat every word it hears." Larry bought the bird but found it would not speak a word. Nevertheless, the clerk told the truth. Can you explain?

Over a two-week period a man and woman made a series of bets on what the stock market would do. At the end of the two weeks the man counted his winnings. At $1.00 per bet, the woman owed the man one times two times three times four times five times six times seven times eight times nine times zero dollars. How much did the man win?

---

2. Create some of your own "guess the pattern" games. Try the games out on your friends. If they give up, give them clues.

3. Reflect on this exercise by responding to the following questions: Which patterns were the easiest to find? Which were more difficult? Which were frustrating? What discoveries did you make about yourself and your capacity to find or create patterns? What ideas do you have about how you can continue to work on strengthening this logical-mathematical capacity?

Answers to "Guess the Pattern" Games

Numbers—Each new number is the result of adding the three previous numbers.

Words—Divide the alphabet in half (*A–L, M–Z*). The first word begins with *A* and the second with *L;* first and last letters of the first half of the alphabet. The third word begins with *M* and the fourth with *Z,* (the first and last letters of the second half of the alphabet). The pattern then proceeds with words that start with *B* and *K,* and *N* and *Y* the second letters.

Visual Symbols—The pattern repeats the final symbol then returns to the first symbol and continues.

Word Problems—80 minutes = 1 hour, 20 minutes; either Larry can't talk or the parrot can't hear; the man won nothing.

Exercise 2: Finding Natural Patterns

1. For one week become a pattern-finding detective. Your job is to find as many *naturally occurring* patterns as you can in your life and environment. Record your findings in a chart. Use the following to get you started, but feel free to add columns and rows as you discover new patterns: patterns you find in nature, patterns of a pet that you own, patterns related to your body, patterns of the food you eat, patterns of the weather for the week, auditory patterns in nature, color and texture patterns of a favorite spot, routine patterns of various family members.

2. At the end of the week, look over the chart for any recurring or similar patterns in the first column; for example, a spiral pattern you found in nature may also be in your food and in the colors or textures in your favorite spot. See how many patterns you can find that recur in at least three different categories.

3. Reflect on this exercise by responding to the following questions: Which pattern stands out? Which were the most interesting? Most surprising? What have you learned about the patterns that are part of your life? What new discoveries have you made? If you were to give the list a title that embodies what you've discovered about patterns, you would call it _____

Musical-Rhythmic Intelligence

The Impact of Sound

How Sound Are You?

> *Of the seven intelligences, the musical-rhythmic may have the most power to change our consciousness. We can use music, rhythm, and sound to instantly change our moods and shift our awareness. Sounds can soothe us, awaken forgotten memories, create anxiety, or cause intense irritation.*

Phase 1: The Impact of Sound on the Psyche

Getting Started
You will need a radio or a CD player in which a friend has loaded a wide variety of music disks. Program the CD player for random play.

Basic Process
This exercise asks you to listen to a wide range of musical, rhythmic, tonal, and vibrational patterns and to reflect on their impact on you.

Listening Exercise
1. Turn on your radio and "cruise" the channels until you hear some music. Listen to the piece that is playing. When it is over, find another piece and listen until it is over, then move on to the next station. Or start the CD player on random play and listen to each selection. Continue until you have listened to approximately ten different pieces. You don't have to listen to the whole piece once you have experienced enough to feel its impact on you.

2. On a chart with the headings, *What emotions does it evoke? What is my physical response to it? What does it make me think of?* analyze the impact of the various pieces on you.

3. Refer to the chart as you answer these questions: What do you notice? Where do you see the biggest differences? Where do you see similarities? As you look over the chart, what surprises you? What is most interesting? Disturbing? Exciting? What types of music produced the strongest responses (positive or negative)? Which produced responses that were fairly neutral? Where do you see patterns in your response to certain types of music, rhythm, and sound? Classify these according to how they affect you.

Phase 2: Shifting Your Awareness with Music, Rhythm, and Sound

Getting Started

You will need a record player, audiocassette player, or CD player; a tape recorder; and several blank tapes. You will also need a variety of music, rhythm, and sounds. Choose the pieces that strongly affected you.

Basic Process

In exercise 1 you create a set of "awareness shifting" tapes. In exercise 2 you learn how to use these tapes to optimize your performance and experience for an upcoming situation.

Exercise 1: Strategic Sound Planning

1. Think about a typical week of your life. Think about the situations in which you find yourself—situations that require a certain frame of mind, a specific mood, or a certain level of awareness for you to be at your best.

2. Create a chart with the headings *Situation, My Typical Response,* and *My Desired Response.* List the situations in the first column of the chart. Analyze each situation under the appropriate headings.

3. Review the reflections you made in phase 1. Then look at what you have written in the last column of the chart and select a type of music, rhythm, or sound that you think would help you shift your mood to your desired state.

4. For each desired state, record several selections that will help you achieve that state. Label each tape according to the situation it is intended to help you with (for example, "music for promoting creative thinking," "music to get me out of the doldrums").

Exercise 2: Applying the Sound Strategies

During the coming week, experiment with using the tapes. Try two strategies.

1. Before entering one of the situations you listed on the chart, play the tape that you recorded to help you shift to the ideal state. As you listen

to the music, relax and allow it to have its effect. Reflect on the effect that it is having. As you enter the situation, maintain the state of being you have achieved while you listened to the tape. While you are in the situation, if you feel yourself losing the desired state of being, pause for a moment and hear the music playing in your head. Reestablish the desired state.

2. After being in a situation in which you experienced a less-than-ideal state, play a tape to help you shift to the ideal. As you listen to the music, relax and allow it to have its effect. Reflect on the effect that it is having. Reflect on the situation and think about what happened to cause this less-than-ideal state. List the factors that seem to affect you. Next time you find yourself in this situation, pause for a moment and try to hear the appropriate music playing in your head.

Exploring the Musical-Rhythmic Motifs of Your Life

My Life Is Alive with the Sound of Music

> *In this powerful practice you have the opportunity to tell your life story through rhythm and sound. This exercise will take you to the heart of the unique, expressive language of musical-rhythmic intelligence.*

The Sound Track of Your Life

Getting Started

You will need a record player, audiocassette player, or CD player; a tape recorder and blank tapes; and a variety of music to record.

Basic Process

In the first exercise you create a time line of your life's journey to the present. In the second exercise you think of various musical, rhythmic, and auditory associations that could represent the various phases of your life and create a recording of these pieces.

Exercise 1: Charting Your Life's Journey

Note: This process is identical to "Reenacting Your Life's Journey" in the bodily-kinesthetic chapter. See pages 10–11 for directives.

Exercise 2: Orchestrating Your Life's Journey

1. Use a chart with the headings *Name of the Stage, Emotion/Feeling of the Stage, Musical Associations with the Stage, Rhythmic Associations with the Stage,* and *Sound/Auditory Associations with the Stage,* to analyze the various stages of your life via music, rhythm, and sound. You don't have to have something on the chart for every category if nothing comes to you. Trust your intuition.

   In column 1, write the name of each stage of your life from the time line work sheet. In column 2, list various emotions or feelings you associate with each stage. In column 3, brainstorm various kinds of music and specific musical pieces you associate with each stage. In column 4, brainstorm rhythmic patterns you associate with each stage. In column five, brainstorm sounds you associate with each stage.

2. Your task is to create an audiocassette that tells the story of your life through music, rhythm, and sound only. This project may take several weeks. Schedule several time slots during the next few weeks when you can work on the tape. Don't try to complete the tape in one sitting. You don't have to proceed sequentially. Let your work grow naturally, at its own speed, in its own order.

   Use the following guidelines in any way that is helpful to you.

   ◆ **Brainstorm a variety of sounds** for each stage. Include environmental, human, mechanically or electronically produced sounds, and instrument sounds.

   ◆ **Compile recorded items** that "speak to you" about the various stages.

   ◆ **Create an outline of what will be included** on the various sections of the tape. The title for the tape will be whatever you choose to title your life's journey to the present. The section titles should be the same as the titles you have given each stage.

   ◆ **Begin recording when you are ready.** Do not use spoken words (although you may need to include some vocal sounds). Later you will have an opportunity to write interpretive or contextual information to go with the tape.

   ◆ **When you have recorded a given stage, listen to it** and ask yourself, "Does this adequately communicate *for me* this stage of my life's journey?" If not, "What additions or deletions are needed?"

   ◆ **Rerecord anything that needs changing.**

   ◆ **When the entire recording is complete, create the inside jacket for the tape.** Write various words of explanation and interpretation that might help someone else grasp your creative process (whether or not you ever allow someone else to hear it). The labeling process will help you bring closure to the exercise.

   ◆ *If it is appropriate for you,* **ask a trusted friend to listen to your tape and share with you its impact.**

3. Reflect on the process of creating this tape and on your finished product. What parts are most memorable for you? What parts of the tape stand out in your mind? What surprised you? What was most interesting? Which part of the process was most engaging for you? What was most valuable to you? What did you learn about yourself as you were creating the tape? What did you learn about yourself from your tape?

My Auditory Environment

Shhhhh! Listen! What Do You Hear?

> *Every day we are bombarded with hundreds of different sounds. Each of these has an obvious or subtle impact on us. This practice builds your capacity to hear sounds in your surroundings, to learn from these sounds, and to make adjustments to your auditory environment.*

Phase 1: Sensitivity to Sound

Getting Started

Complete each of the exercises within a week. Plan at least five slots of time for the first exercise and four for the second. Each phase of each exercise requires a minimum of ten minutes.

Basic Process

Exercise 1 helps you intensify your sense of hearing by practicing "magnified hearing" in a variety of situations. Exercise 2 fine-tunes some of the more subtle aspects of this auditory intelligence.

Exercise 1: Awareness of the Impact of Sound

1. Think of five places that have very different kinds of sounds (for example, a busy street in the city, a secluded area in a forest, your living room). Select places that have a wide variety of sounds and rhythms. Plan to visit each place when you have time simply to be there and listen.

2. Spend at least ten minutes sitting quietly in each environment, simply listening. Pretend that your sense of hearing is attached to the volume knob on a radio and that you can turn it up at will.

3. Reproduce the following chart five times and record your auditory observations and experiences in the various environments you have chosen. For level 1, close your eyes and listen. What has an immediate impact on you? For level 2, imagine that you can turn up your hearing. With eyes closed, listen for what you didn't hear at the previous level. For level 3, turn up your hearing even further. What do you hear now that escaped you at the previous levels? After each level of listening, record the sounds you heard, their emotional impact on you, and what the various sounds tell you about what is happening in your environment.

Environment:			
Hearing Level 1: *Listen to the obvious, immediately accessible sounds*	What sounds do I hear?	What feelings do they evoke?	What's happening? What's going on?
Hearing Level 2: *Listen for the more subtle, less obvious sounds*	What sounds do I hear?	What feelings do they evoke?	What's happening? What's going on?
Hearing Level 3: *Listen for the sounds that are beyond this immediate situation*	What sounds do I hear?	What feelings do they evoke?	What's happening? What's going on?

4. Look at the five charts from your five listening experiences and answer the following questions: What immediately grabs your attention? Which responses appear on more than one chart? Which are on only one? What do you see that surprises you? What is most interesting? What is confusing? What bothers or disturbs you? What patterns do you see? What have you learned about yourself by doing this exercise? What new insights do you have about your sense of hearing?

Exercise 2: Tuning in to Subtle Sounds

For each of the following situations turn up your hearing capabilities as you did in the previous exercise.

Note: After each miniexercise, spend a few minutes reflecting on your experience using the questions on page 81.

Breathing

Notice the breathing patterns or rhythms of various people. Try to classify them, for example, the breathing that is like a steady march, the breathing that is like going to sleep. Listen to the different kinds of sighs. What different types do you notice (for example, the "I'm bored" sigh, the "I'm contented" sigh, or the "I'm impatient" sigh)?

Bodily Sounds

Listen for the voluntary sounds that communicate a general state of being, for example, the sound of frequent shifting of position, the tapping of a foot. Tune in to bodily sounds that are less voluntary, such as the growling stomach, the suppressed belch, the yawn.

Footsteps

Sit on a park bench and close your eyes. Listen to the various walking and running patterns you hear from passersby. How would you classify them in terms of what you intuit the various people are doing? Sit in the lobby of an office building or hotel and close your eyes. Notice the various styles of walking that you hear. What do you think each person is feeling? Sit in a hallway of a hospital or social service agency and close your eyes. Again listen to the footsteps you hear. What do they tell you is going on?

Silence

Close your eyes, and first become aware of the subtle sounds of this space (for example, the hum of the air conditioning, the sound of the weather). Relax and focus on the sounds you are making as you sit (for example, the sounds of your body and clothing as you adjust your posture, your breathing, your heartbeat).

The Inner World

Focus on your inner world and listen with "subtle ears." What is your experience of this inner world? What do you sense? Imagine that you can turn up the volume of this inner world. What do you hear that you didn't hear before? What do you feel? See if you can hear the inner beat and rhythm of the life force as it flows through you.

MiniExercise Reflection Questions

- What did I notice? What did I hear? What really grabbed my attention?

- What did I hear that surprised me? Which sounds were most fascinating to me? Which were irritating? Which sounds were calming? Which were humorous? Which were boring?

- What sounds affected me more than others? Am I aware of any patterns in how various sounds affect me?

- What sounds did I hear that are always there but I've not been aware of before?

Creating Music, Rhythm, and Sound

*I've got rhythm;
I've got music.
Who could ask for
anything more?*

> *When we hear certain musical pieces, we are often transported to other times and places. Various rhythms and beats can evoke emotional and physical responses in us. Certain sounds can conjure up images and experiences. Think of radio shows such as "The Shadow" or the drum-roll at the circus when a performer is about to try a difficult feat.*

Phase 1: Sound Associations

Getting Started

For the first exercise you need audiotapes or CDs of three old-time radio shows. Try to find a variety (for example, a comedy, a thriller, a western). For the second exercise you need to record several TV shows on a VCR.

Basic Process

In these exercises you explore the sound components of various entertainment experiences as well as of your everyday life. You focus on what are usually unconscious aspects of these experiences.

Exercise 1: Special Effects of Old-Time Radio Shows

1. Listen to three different old-time radio programs and, on three sheets of paper, answer the following questions to analyze each sound track. Focus primarily on how the sound track illustrates and enhances your experience of the verbal aspects of the program.

    ◆ *How is music used to help create the story?*

        ▶ When and how is the theme song used?

        ▶ What types of music are used to increase the suspense? To emphasize humor? To signal danger? To indicate a chase or a fight?

        ▶ What kinds of music are used for transitions between scenes?

► Is there music that signals "the end," "to be continued," or "and now, back to our story"?

♦ ***What are the special sound effects and how does each affect you?***

► What happens in your imagination when you hear certain sounds?

► What physical responses do you have when you hear certain sounds?

► What sounds cause you to make a sound?

► What other senses are stimulated by the sounds?

♦ ***What vocal techniques are employed to enhance the story?***

► How do actors communicate emotion?

► What effect does the rhythm of their speaking have on the story?

► When do they speak very slowly or very rapidly?

► How do they use silence?

► How do the actors use accents or unique pronunciations to help you visualize the story?

2. Place the sound analyses from the three programs side by side so that you can compare them.

> **Highlight the following items with a colored marker:** similar patterns of music, similar patterns of sound effects, and similar patterns of the human voice.

> **With a different colored marker, highlight the following items:** patterns of music being used for **similar purposes,** patterns of sound effects being used for **similar purposes,** and voice patterns being used for **similar purposes?**

> **With a third marker, highlight these items:** patterns of music being used for **different purposes,** patterns of sound effects being used for **different purposes,** and voice patterns being used for **different purposes?**

Exercise 2: TV Sound Effects

1. In this exercise you have a visual way to check your "sound intuitions" and responses. Begin by selecting three types of TV shows (for example, a sitcom, a detective show, and a drama). Set up your VCR to record the selected programs. Then cover the screen or adjust the knobs so that you can hear the sound but not see the picture.

2. Listen to at least a ten-minute segment of each program and use the questions from the previous exercise (page 82) to analyze the sound tracks.

3. After you have completed the "sound analysis" for each program, check the accuracy of your auditory sensitivity by watching the segments that you recorded. Where were your observations on target? Where were your observations inaccurate? What did you miss in the sound track that could have clued you in to what was happening? If this program were to be turned into a radio show, what elements of the sound track would need to change so that the listener could fully experience the program through sound alone?

Phase 2: Weaving New Sound Associations

Getting Started

For each exercise you need recording equipment, and for exercises 1 and 3, you also need the help of a friend. Each exercise requires some time for brainstorming, time for gathering the appropriate auditory props, and time for recording.

Basic Process

The first exercise enhances your awareness of everyday sounds. In the second exercise you experiment with using music, rhythm, and sounds to represent your experience of a typical day, as well as how you could use sounds to enhance your experience. The third exercise enlarges your experience of written information using music, rhythm, and sound.

Exercise 1: The Sound Track of Everyday Happenings

1. For each of the following situations describe the kind of music (or a specific piece) that would be appropriate in the background, a rhythm or beat that could communicate what is happening, and any other sounds that would amplify the experience: stuck in rush hour traffic; a child's first steps; unexpectedly seeing your girlfriend or boyfriend; holding a cuddly, warm puppy; an assignment you hate; the beginning of spring; the start of the weekend; your favorite holiday season; summer vacation; a shopping trip. and relaxing in a favorite spot in nature.

2. Select at least four situations and create a tape recording to communicate the experience through music, rhythm, and sound. Then listen to each segment of your tape and evaluate its evocative power—does it communicate what you intended?

3. Play your recording for a friend. Share your list of the situations above and ask this person to guess which experience you were trying to represent. Have your friend give you feedback. What music, rhythms, and sounds are exactly what your friend would have included on the tape to communicate the experience? What would your friend add to the tape to more fully communicate the experience? You may find it interesting to play your tape for several people and compare their responses.

4. Reflect, using these questions: What did you find most interesting about step 1? What were the most striking similarities and differences among your own and others' choices? What have you learned about yourself and your auditory process? What other dimensions of your auditory experience would you like to explore at some time in the future?

Exercise 2: The Sound Effects of Everyday Life

1. Think about your typical workday and divide it into four parts: before school, during school, after school, and in the evening. Using a chart, reflect on each part of the day. List normal events, typical mood, physical state, and what you're usually thinking.

2. Now reflect on what you have recorded. List a theme song, rhythm, and background sounds for each time of day.

3. Close your eyes and see if you can hear the appropriate music, rhythm, or sounds for each segment of the day. What do you hear?

4. Think about changes you would like to make in how you experience a typical day. What would be ideal? Reflect on how music, rhythm, and sound can help alter your experience. Brainstorm theme songs, rhythms, and background sounds that might help you shift your experiences to more optimal experiences.

5. Create an audiotape that includes the optimal elements. For at least one week, experiment with playing this tape at the beginning of each day. Reflect on how it changes your experience and your ability to cope with the events of the day.

Exercise 3: Illustrating the Written Word with Sound

1. Choose a passage from a favorite story.

2. Read the selection and imagine that you are producing this story as a radio drama. Consider the following elements to enhance the listener's experience of the story. What elements of sound would help the listener visualize what is happening? What variations in tone, pitch, and rhythm are needed for the characters? Where could music be added to help create the various moods of each part of the story?

3. Record the story, incorporating the ideas you have brainstormed.

4. Ask a friend to read the story silently. Then play the tape and ask your friend to give you feedback on how the auditory additions enhanced the story.

5. At other times, repeat this process using the following: a news article, a favorite piece of poetry, the description of a product from an advertisement, the instructions for operating your VCR, your favorite recipe, a magazine interview, and a sports writer's description of a game.

6. Reflect on the exercise by answering the following questions: Which parts of the exercise were most memorable? What did you notice? What did you enjoy the most? What was most challenging? What was exciting? What surprised you? What part was most intriguing? What was easy? What was very difficult? What key discoveries did you make? What associations do you see between this exercise and your everyday life? What are other ways you could use this exercise?

Speaking Musically

How Do I Say What I Say?

> *Can you think of times when you were talking with another person and the tone, pitch, and rhythm of her speaking didn't match her words? Maybe a teacher announced that she would talk about something very exciting but then droned on in a monotone. Or maybe you were talking with a friend about a controversial topic and he assured you in an emphatic way, "No! I am not upset by what you just said!!!" Often how we say what we say communicates more than our actual words.*

The Music and Rhythm of Communication

Getting Started

Each pair of exercises (1 and 2, 3 and 4) requires part of a weekend day for preparation, a week at work for observation of others and yourself, and part of an additional weekend day for processing and reflection. You need to enlist a friend to help you with the processing stages, and you also need a tape recorder.

Basic Process

In exercises 1 and 2 you analyze the tonal aspects of verbal communication, and in 3 and 4, the rhythmic aspects. Try to perform each set of exercises in consecutive weeks, for each builds on the experience of the previous set.

Exercise 1: The Tonal Qualities of Communication

1. Spend a couple of evenings watching a variety of TV shows and analyze the **tonal qualities** of the dialogue. See if you can recognize and associate certain vocal tonal patterns with the following: sarcasm, empathy, happiness, sadness, irritation, sincerity, surprise, boredom, contentment, affection, sympathy, and determination

2. Over the course of several days, listen carefully to the tones of people's communication with one another. See if you can hear the same qualities that you did when you were analyzing the TV shows. When you recognize the tonal pattern, list it on a sheet of paper.

Intelligence Builders for Every Student © 1998 Zephyr Press, Tucson, AZ

3. Over the course of several days, listen carefully to the tones of your own communication with others. See if you can detect the same tonal qualities that you noticed when you were analyzing the TV shows. When you recognize the tonal pattern, list it on a sheet of paper.

4. Reflect on this exercise by answering the following questions: What really stands out? What do you find most interesting? Most surprising? Most entertaining? Most disturbing? What have you learned about the role of tonal patterns in the art of communication?

Exercise 2: The Strategic Use of Tonal Patterns

1. Get a box of pasta, oats, or other product with the cooking instructions on the box.

2. Turn on a tape recorder, then read the instructions at least twelve times, trying to embody fully all the tonal qualities you identified in the last exercise.

3. Play the tape for a friend. Give your friend the list of emotions and see if he can identify each based on the tones you used.

4. Ask your friend to give you feedback on your "performance." For any your friend didn't get "right," ask him to direct you (as in a Broadway play) to more fully embody those emotions in your voice. Ask your friend to coach you on any that he feels could be improved to express more fully the emotion you intended to convey.

5. Repeat this process with two other friends. Note those areas where your communication seems to be consistent and clear and those that are ambiguous or confused.

6. List at least five areas of your daily communication that this exercise calls to mind, areas which you need to improve.

Exercise 3: The Beat, Rhythm, and Vibration of Communication

1. The next two exercises mirror the previous two; however, you deal with the rhythm, beat, vibration, and all the sounds of communication.

2. Once again, spend a couple of evenings watching a variety of TV shows. This time listen to and analyze the rhythmic and vibrational patterns of the dialogue and the accompanying sound effects. As much as possible ignore the pitch and tone of people's voices. Try to focus on and identify vocal rhythmic and vibrational patterns that are part of effective communication (for example, speaking in a fast staccato fashion or very slowly, as if there is all the time in the world).

Use the following list to help you recognize and identify the various beats, rhythms, and vibrations that underlie human communication: communicates tension or anxiety, communicates nonchalance, communicates fear or terror, communicates well-being, communicates frivolity, communicates boredom, communicates urgency, communicates excitement, and communicates anger or hostility.

3. Over the course of several days, listen carefully to the rhythmic and vibrational aspects of people's communication with one another. See if you can hear the same patterns that you observed in the various TV shows. When you can recognize the rhythmic pattern, list it on a sheet of paper.

4. Over the course of several days, listen carefully to the rhythmic and vibrational aspects of your own communication with others. See if you can detect the same patterns as you did in the TV shows. When you can recognize the rhythmic pattern, list it on a sheet of paper.

5. Reflect on this exercise by answering the following questions: What really stands out? What do you find most interesting? Most surprising? Most entertaining? Most disturbing? What have you learned about the role rhythmic and vibrational patterns play in the art of communication?

Exercise 4: The Strategic Use of Beat, Rhythm, and Vibration in Communication

1. Select two or three patterns that you know well, for example, the ABCs, counting to 50 by 2s, states and their capitols.

2. Turn on a tape recorder and recite these patterns at least nine times, trying to embody fully the various beats, rhythms, and vibrations you identified in the last exercise to communicate the moods or emotions. As much as possible try to maintain a neutral tone so that the rhythmic pattern is emphasized.

3. Play the tape for a friend. Give your friend the list of emotions and see if she can identify each based on the rhythmic and vibrational patterns you used.

4. Ask your friend to give you feedback on your "performance." For any patterns your friend didn't get "right," ask her to direct you in how to embody more fully the various emotions or moods in the rhythmic patterns of your speaking. In the same manner, ask your friend to coach you on any that she feels could be improved to express more fully the emotion or mood you intended.

5. Repeat this process with two other friends. Note those areas where your verbal, rhythmic communication seems to be consistent and clear, and where it is ambiguous or confused.

6. List at least five areas of your daily communication that this exercise calls to mind and that require some change.

Listening with the Whole Body

Groovin' on a Sunday Afternoon

> *Music, rhythm, and sound are powerful tools. Think about experiences of sound that touch us so deeply they produce physical changes in the body. Certain music can move us to tears. Certain sounds can produce a quickened heartbeat. Certain rhythms cause us to tap our feet or get up and dance. Some sounds are irritating and make us want to get away from them; others produce feelings of relaxation, peace, and calm.*

Phase 1: Listening and Hearing with the Whole Body

Getting Started

For the first exercise you'll need a boom box and a piece of music with a strong beat. You also need a space where you can be alone and where loud music will not disturb others.

Basic Process

In the first exercise you experiment with feeling the vibration of music in various regions of your body. The second exercise asks you to experiment with sounds you make with your vocal chords, again noticing the impact in various parts of your body.

Exercise 1: Sensing Sound and Vibrations in the Body (external)

1. Choose a piece of music with a distinct beat, and find a place where you can play this music very loudly.

2. Play the music. Listen to it for a couple minutes, then turn up the volume. Continue listening for another couple minutes, then turn up the volume again and listen for a couple more minutes.

3. Plug your ears and listen to the music for two to three minutes. What is different between hearing the music directly and hearing it through plugged ears? Go back and forth between open ears and plugged ears to notice everything.

4. Find a way to plug your ears so that your hands are free. Play the music loudly and place your hands on the boom box. Feel the vibrations of the music on your hands. See how low you can turn the volume and still feel the vibrations. Continue for at least five minutes.

5. Reflect, using the following questions: What are your observations about this experience? What was surprising? Interesting? What did you sense about the music?

6. Keeping your ears plugged and moving the boom box as necessary, lie down on the ground and place the speakers near your abdomen. Turn the sound up loud enough that you feel the vibrations in your abdomen for at least five minutes.

7. Repeat step 5.

8. Repeat the process with other parts of your body.

9. Repeat step 5 after each body part.

Exercise 2: Sensing Sound and Vibrations in the Body (internal)

1. Hum in a pitch that creates a strong vibration in your head. Close first your right ear, then your left. Note any differences you experience. Then close both ears and notice how the humming is different.

2. Once you have found a pitch, tone, and volume that creates the most vibration, spend some time humming and noticing the impact on you.

3. Experiment with moving this experience of sound and vibration into other parts of the body. Plug both ears, close your eyes, and hum. Move the sensing of the sound and vibration to the top of your head. Experiment with various humming volumes until you can feel it there. Sense the sound and vibration in your throat, again experimenting with volume. Move the sound or vibration to the region of the heart. Keep experimenting, moving the experience to other regions of your body.

4. Reflect on the excercises by answering the following questions: What did you find most interesting? Most surprising? What did you observe about how the sound and vibration of the humming affected each part of your body? Where was the impact the strongest? Where could you sense it only remotely? Where could you not sense it at all? What did you learn about yourself and the impact of sound and vibration?

Phase 2: Extraordinary Hearing and Listening

Getting Started

You need a boom box and a piece of music, preferably one that is not familiar to you. It should contain sections with a variety of rhythms, pitches, tones, and so on. You'll probably need about one hour of uninterrupted time to perform this exercise the first time.

Basic Process

Listen to a piece of music until you are thoroughly absorbed in it, then extend this experience into all of your senses. Read over the procedures before you begin so that you can move through the phases of the exercise smoothly.

Exercise: Listening and Hearing with All the Senses

1. Lie on the floor with the boom box above your head. Close your eyes, take several deep breaths, and relax fully. Keep breathing deeply until you sense a deep relaxation throughout your body.

2. Turn on the music, softly at first, but gradually increase the volume until it is at a comfortable level and loud enough that it commands your full sense of hearing.

3. With your eyes still closed, imagine that the music is a stream of warm water or air flowing over, under, and all around you. Imagine that it is caressing your entire body. It is moving in you and through you. Get a sense of the music playing through you as if you were a large, living speaker.

4. When you have a sense of being a speaker, start to focus your attention on your different senses, giving at least three minutes of concentration to each sense. With your eyes closed, see the music and the rhythm. What patterns, shapes, objects, colors, and so on does the music evoke? Are the images abstract or realistic? Taste the music and the rhythm. Is the music sweet or bitter? Hot or spicy or bland? Smell the music and the rhythm. Allow them to evoke odors. Do you smell a fresh, clean smell or a stale smell? Maybe you sense the aroma of flowers or a favorite food. Finally, experiment with touching the music and the rhythm. Run your hands over the various textures that the music evokes. Do you feel velvet or sandpaper? Hard or soft? What is the temperature?

5. Slowly turn down the volume until the music is off. Lie quietly for a few minutes enjoying the feelings and thoughts.

6. Reflect on the exercise by answering the following questions: What do you remember most? Which of the senses produced the most vivid experience? Which one was most difficult for you to access? What do you find surprising? What was most interesting? What new discoveries did you make about yourself? What did you get out of the piece that you probably would not have if you'd approached it only through hearing? What other things would you like to do with this exercise?

Phase 3: Using Sound to Alter the Body

Getting Started

For the first exercise you need another person. You also need an audiocassette player, a large sheet of blank paper, and a variety of colors of highlighter pens. For the second exercise you need an audiocassette recorder, a blank tape, and a second audiocassette or CD player. You'll also need a wide selection of recorded music.

Exercise 1: The Physical Effects of Sound

1. Ask a friend to record a wide variety of sounds. Your friend should include soothing sounds as well as irritating sounds, sounds from nature, from machines, from animals and humans. Some should be very loud and others barely audible, some startling and others boring. Each sound segment should last at least two minutes, with approximately thirty seconds between segments.

2. When your friend has finished recording, find out how many sound segments are on the tape and then divide a large sheet of paper into this number of sections.

3. Play the tape fairly loudly and observe yourself. For each sound segment, ask yourself, "What is my body's reaction to this sound?" Every time you are aware of a physical response, write down the effect the sound is having on you. Stay focused on physical responses; don't worry about thoughts and opinions.

4. Look back over the reactions you recorded. Using several highlighter pens, mark responses that are similar.

5. Use a chart with the headings, *Describe the physical response, Summarize the kinds of sounds that caused it,* and *When do I experience this in everyday life?* to classify and analyze your highlighted responses.

6. Reflect on the exercise by referring to your chart and answering the following questions: What was most memorable? What catches your attention? What do you find most interesting? What surprises you about the classification and analysis? What did you discover about the impact of sound on yourself? What is disturbing? How can you use this information to help you in your daily life?

Exercise 2: Altering the Body with Music, Rhythm, and Sound

1. Create a chart with the names of the parts of your day as headings. Divide your day into five parts. In the first row, describe the physical state you think would be optimal for each part of the day. In the second row, brainstorm specific pieces of music, certain kinds of sounds, or distinct rhythmic patterns you think could help you achieve this optimal state.

2. Create a master tape that contains specific pieces of music and sounds. Start with five tapes to make it easier to make alterations. Record at least a ten-minute segment for each part of the day. Each segment may be a single piece or a variety of music, sounds, and beats that help you optimize your physical state. This process may be lengthy. Give yourself plenty of time to find and record exactly what you need.Once you feel each segment is right, you may record a single master tape.

3. Use your tape. Work with one segment until you know how to make it work for you, then move to another segment. Be patient with yourself. Let the body respond to the tape on its own. If your body tells you that a particular sound isn't right, feel free to record a new segment on the tape.

4. Work with the tape for several weeks, paying close attention to how sound can help you change physical responses.

Using Music, Rhythm, and Sound to Enhance Learning and Living

The music's gonna move ya!
The rhythm's gonna get ya!

> *Music, rhythm, and sound are an important part of our daily lives. In early childhood we learned many things through music, such as the ABCs. Music can accelerate learning by modulating the electrical patterns of the brain. Music also has the power to provoke profound levels of creativity in us.*

Phase 1: Using Music to Enhance Learning and Expand Creativity

Getting Started

For the second exercise you need a recording of a favorite piece of instrumental music, a large piece of blank paper, and a set of colored markers.

Basic Process

In the first exercise you adapt various songs and rhythms to help you recall information. The second exercise has you experiment with music to spark your creativity.

Exercise 1: Music and Rhythm as Mnemonic Devices

1. List pieces of information that you sometimes need to know and that you have difficulty remembering, for example: *birthdays or anniversaries, directions for getting to a particular place,* or *vocabulary words.*

2. List some of your favorite songs, tunes, and rhythmic patterns.

3. Select an item from step 1 and try to fit it into one of the songs or rhythmic patterns in step 2. Work with it until it flows nicely, the words rhyme appropriately, and it is fun to sing and easy to remember. Practice the song or pattern until you have it memorized.

Exercise 2: Music, Rhythm, and Sound as Creativity Enhancements

Drawing to Music

See what creative shapes, patterns, doodles, or pictures music can evoke in you.

1. Select a favorite piece of **instrumental** music that contains a range of tones, pitches, rhythms, and volumes.

2. Find a space with ample room for you to lay out various drawing materials: colored markers, pencils, chalk, and several large sheets of paper. This place should also be one where you will not be disturbed for about twenty minutes. Play the music louder than you would normally so it has a strong impact.

3. As you listen, choose the appropriate marker, pencil, or chalk that you feel matches the mood of the music. Imagine that the music is flowing into your arm and hand, making you draw shapes, squiggles, symbols, or other images.

4. When the mood of the music changes, change colors. Allow rhythm changes to change what you are drawing. Express loudness and softness in your drawing.

5. When the music ends, replay the piece. Focus on your drawing and see if you can recognize the various parts that relate to the various aspects of the music.

6. Turn off the music and reflect on what you have created by answering the following questions: What immediately grabs your attention? What shapes and patterns are most dramatic? Which are more subtle? What in the color schemes strikes you? Which parts of your drawing do you really like? Which part is most intriguing? What delights you? What surprises you? What do you find amusing? What title would you give this creation? Imagine that the drawing is displayed in an art museum and you are an art critic: Where in this drawing do you see a strong expression of the artist's emotional response (either positive or negative)?

Writing with Music

1. List ten recent meaningful experiences in your life. Choose one to write about.

2. Select a piece of **instrumental** music that you feel in some way reflects this event or your feelings about it.

3. Find a quiet space with a desk or table for writing. This place should also be one where you will not be disturbed for about twenty minutes. Play the music louder than usual so that it is more than simply background music.

4. Close your eyes and visualize the experience as vividly as you can, allowing the music to take you back to the experience. When you feel ready, start writing about the experience as if you were writing in a

Intelligence Builders for Every Student © 1998 Zephyr Press, Tucson, AZ

journal. Pause frequently and listen to the music, allowing it to help you reconnect with some of the emotions or some of the extraordinary dimensions of this experience.

5. Write at least three paragraphs about the experience, reflecting on it from many different angles. Allow the music to evoke various metaphors or wild descriptions that you might not normally permit yourself to express.

6. Turn off the music and read aloud what you have written. Reflect on your writing by answering the following questions: What words, phrases, or sentences really strike you? Which parts do you really like? What is most interesting? What delights you? What surprises you? What is moving? What is amusing? What connections do you see between what you have written and other aspects of your life? What title would you give this composition? Imagine that you are a literary critic writing a review of this composition. What are the strong features of this author's creative writing abilities? What is the underlying message this author is trying to communicate through this essay?

Thinking through Music

Experiment with music as a means to enhance and intensify your thinking process.

1. For each of the following, recall a recent experience of being in that situation and think of a piece of music that might have helped your thinking processes: solving a difficult problem, getting yourself out of a depression, being innovative or creative, dealing with anger, frustration, disappointment, and meeting a new challenge.

2. Gather the musical selections you have listed and carry them with you during the next two to three weeks. As often as possible, play the music just before those situations for which you need to prepare or just after those situations for which you need a shift in awareness.

3. Reflect by answering the following questions: What are your immediate impressions? What new feelings or emotions were you aware of? What interested you? What was surprising? In which situation did the music produce the most dramatic effects? In which were the effects minimal? What did you learn about how music can help you get into a better frame of mind for coping with and thinking about life? What other situations could be positively enhanced by adding music to them?

Phase 2: Music and Rhythm and the Accelerated Learning Process*

Getting Started

For the exercise you need a tape recorder and a CD or tape player. Record a set of facts, procedures, or other information you need to commit to memory. You also need a tape or CD of baroque largos or adagios.

*Adapted from Lazear, David. 1991. *Sevens Ways of Knowing: Teaching for Multiple Intelligences* (Palatine, Ill.: Skylight).

Basic Process

The exercise starts with helping you get into an alpha state of awareness using the baroque music. While listening to the music, you play the recorded information in the background.

Exercise: An Experiment in Superlearning

1. Brainstorm a list of facts, figures, procedures, or other information you need or want to commit to memory. Tape record this information slowly three times.

2. Sit in a comfortable chair, lie on a carpeted floor, or get comfortable. Spend a few minutes relaxing, making sure that you focus on relaxing each part of your body.

3. Play the baroque music. Let the music carry you for a few minutes. Use it to help you relax more.

4. With the music still playing, play the audiocassette on which you recorded the information to memorize. As the information is being played, keep your primary attention on the music; the information tape is the background for the music.

5. When the information tape is finished playing, let the music continue for a few more minutes. Slowly bring yourself back to a more ordinary state of awareness. Test yourself on the information you were trying to learn. What do you notice about this way of taking in information?

Researchers have observed that people who regularly use such techniques learn material at significantly accelerated rates.

Phase 3: Music, Rhythm, and Sound Meditations

Getting Started

You need three tapes or CDs, one of relaxation music (preferably music that has no identifiable tune or something that is unfamiliar), one of percussion instruments (American Indian drumming or the drums of Africa are good), and one of environmental sounds.

Basic Process

These exercises give you meditation or concentration practices using music, rhythm, and sound. Each asks you to listen to various musical tones, rhythmic and vibrational patterns, and sounds, and then use them to help you journey within. In each experience, simply observe yourself; don't analyze.

Exercise 1: An Experimental Music Meditation

1. Sit in a comfortable chair with the tape or CD player at hand. Have your tape or CD cued and ready to go. Spend a few minutes consciously relaxing. You might try the following process: Close your eyes if doing so seems natural and comfortable to you and take several deep breaths, breathing from your abdomen. Focus your attention on each inhalation and exhalation, using the exhalation to help you relax. Each time you exhale, allow any tension you are experiencing to melt away. Allow any worries to simply drop away for a few minutes. Continue to focus on your breathing and allow your mind to become very still; as fully as you can, bring yourself to this present moment of "just being."

2. While you continue to focus on your breathing, turn on the tape or CD and allow the music to enhance and deepen your relaxation. Allow your breathing to adjust itself naturally to the flow of the music.

3. When you sense a deep, inner calm, focus on the music. What feeling does it evoke in you? What images come to your mind? What associations do you make?

4. After about ten minutes of listening to the music, write a few lines of reflection.

Exercise 2: An Experimental Rhythm Meditation

1. Sit in a comfortable chair with the tape or CD player at hand. Have your rhythm selection cued and ready to go. Spend a few minutes consciously relaxing. You might try the following process: All at once, tense every muscle in your body and hold it for five seconds. Suddenly let go of the tension and notice the contrast. Repeat this process several times, each time allowing yourself to relax more. After several times, close your eyes and simply enjoy the feeling of total body relaxation. Focus on your breathing and allow your mind to become very still. As fully as you can, bring yourself to an awareness of this moment, letting go of any concerns or thoughts.

2. Turn on the tape or CD and allow the beat and vibrations of the recording to surround you.

3. Notice what the rhythms evoke in you. What parts of your physical being respond to the various patterns you hear? What feelings occur? What images come to mind? What thoughts and associations do the rhythms provoke?

4. After about ten minutes of listening to the tape or CD, write a few lines of reflection on your experience.

Exercise 3: An Experimental Sound Meditation

1. Sit in a comfortable chair with the tape or CD player at hand. Have your environmental sound selection cued and ready to go. Spend a few minutes consciously relaxing. You might try the following: Close your eyes, focus on your feet, and consciously relax them. You may need to wiggle your toes and ankles, flexing them several times, then letting go of the tension. Proceed systematically up your body, repeating this process with each part. Spend a couple of minutes enjoying the sensation of total body relaxation. Focus on your breathing and allow your mind to become very still. As fully as you can, bring yourself to an awareness of this moment, letting go of thoughts or concerns.

2. While you continue to focus on your breath, turn on the tape or CD; allow the sounds to transport you in your imagination to the environment you have selected.

3. As you imagine yourself being in this place, pay attention to what the various sounds evoke. What emotional responses are you aware of? What images come to your mind? What associations and experiences do these sounds bring to mind? What thoughts or reflections are evoked?

4. After about ten minutes of listening to the selection, write a few lines of reflection on your experience.

Verbal-Linguistic Intelligence

Speaking What's on Your Mind

Words,
Words,
WORDS,
Words

> Verbal communication is one of our primary ways of interacting with other people. Consider the everyday situations in which you are required to utilize very different modalities of speaking. The following practice works with building a wide range of formal and informal speaking skills. The exercises lead you through experiences of impromptu speaking, persuasive speaking, motivational speaking, and delivering formal presentations.

Formal and Informal Speaking

Basic Process

This exercise is informal.

Exercise 1: Impromptu Speaking Games

The Grab Bag

> ▶ Divide into two teams. Each team places at least ten strange, interesting, or mysterious items into a large paper bag. The more unfamiliar the items, the better!

▶ A person from the first team reaches into the bag prepared by the opposite team and takes out one item. For two minutes, her team brainstorms ten uses for which the item is not generally used.

▶ The person who selected the item presents a three-minute, TV-style advertisement to sell this item, incorporating ideas from the brainstorming session.

▶ Go back and forth between teams until each person has had a turn.

The Random Topic

▶ Each team brainstorms a list of at least ten strange and interesting topics for a speech. They write each topic on a separate slip of paper and include the imagined audience. The stranger the topics and audiences, the better!

▶ A person from the first team draws a slip of paper prepared by the opposite team. For two minutes the team brainstorms the content of the speech.

▶ The person who selected the topic delivers a three-minute speech on the topic to the imagined audience, incorporating ideas from the brainstorming session.

▶ A member of the second team selects a topic from the first team, the team brainstorms, and the person delivers a speech.

▶ The teams take turns until each person has had a turn.

Reflect together on your experience of these games:

What parts do you remember? Are certain lines still ringing in your ears? What was most surprising? Which game did you like more and why? Which was more fun? Most challenging? What did you learn about impromptu speaking? What aspects of impromptu speaking do you feel you need to work on? As a group, brainstorm a list of at least ten everyday situations where you must think on your feet. What are some things you can do that will help you be more comfortable and perform better?

Creative Writing

Juicing Up Your Writing

> *Have you ever marveled at authors who are able to churn out a new novel every five or six months? Do you ever wonder where poets come up with the profound, sometimes outrageous, images they use? How would you keep coming up with creative story lines if you were the writer of a TV sitcom?*

Increasing the Power of Your Written Words

Getting Started

Buy yourself a special notebook for these exercises. Each exercise probably takes about an hour. You can do the exercises on your own or you might find it more fun and interesting to have a friend do them with you.

Exercise 1: Epiphanies of the Moment*

1. Use the "starter phrases" to begin your writing, then write at least ten sentences about each experience, using the ordinary, mundane aspects of the experience, but magnifying them to cosmic, outrageous proportions .

    ◆ *There I was, brushing my teeth, my mouth lathered to overflowing, when in the mirror behind me I saw . . .*

    ◆ *As I stared at the screen of my computer, I was suddenly transported to the magical realm of . . .*

    ◆ *Surrounded by the noise and chatter of the other people on the bus, I found myself strangely detached, speculating . . .*

    ◆ *As I eavesdropped on the conversation at the next table during lunch, I overheard . . .*

    ◆ *There it was, just as I left it, the pile of dirty laundry. As I looked at it, discouraged by its immensity, it started to speak to me, saying . . .*

    ◆ *As I looked at the picture in the magazine, it seemed to come alive and speak to me, saying . . .*

*Adapted from Houston, Jean. 1982. *The Possible Human* (Los Angeles: J. P. Tarcher) and Lazear, David. 1991. *Seven Ways of Knowing: Teaching for Multiple Intelligences* (Palatine, Ill.: Skylight).

2. Read over what you've written and reflect: What words, phrases, or sentences stand out? Which were most fun? Most interesting? Which were very easy to answer? Which sparked bizarre or unexpected responses? Which stretched you or were difficult? What patterns do you notice? What have you learned about your creative writing capacities? How can you adapt this exercise to enhance your creative writing?

Exercise 2: Telling a Good Story*

1. Brainstorm six heroes, villains, settings, conflicts, and endings. Don't ponder; simply list the first six things that pop into your mind.

2. Select one item at random from each category. If you are working with a partner, each of you should randomly select five items.

3. Write an outline for a story that incorporates the five randomly selected items.

4. Tell the story to your partner or, if you have been working alone, find someone to whom you can explain the process, then read your story.

5. Brainstorm several other ways you could use the list to enhance your creative capacities. What adaptations would you need to make to use it in another situation?

Exercise 3: Poetry for Fun

1. Brainstorm at least five news items, typical school experiences, home experiences, and people you meet.

2. Find examples and descriptions of a limerick, a haiku, and a free verse.

3. Select one item from each category in step 1. Assign one poetry form described in step 2 to each selected item.

4. Experiment with writing four different poems using the items and poetic forms you have selected. Be creative, even outrageous. **Don't worry if your poems do not exactly match the descriptions of the poetry forms.**

5. Reflect on the exercise by answering the following questions:

   ◆ What words, phrases, or sentences stand out?

   ◆ Which of the poems do you find most surprising? Most interesting? Most profound? Which was easiest to write? Most difficult?

   ◆ Which form did you find most interesting? What interested you? Which form sparked the greatest creativity in you? Which stretched you?

   ◆ To whom would you read each poem and why would you choose that person or group?

   ◆ How does writing poetry benefit you? What ideas do you have about how poetry writing could become a regular part of your life?

*Adapted from Lazear, David. 1991. *Seven Ways of Knowing: Teaching for Multiple Intelligences* (Palatine, Ill.: Skylight).

Metalinguistic Analysis

Do You Mean What Your Meaning Means to Me?

Analyzing Your Language

Getting Started

You can perform the first exercise alone, with a partner, or with a group. You should do exercises 2, 3, and 4 by yourself. In these exercises you work to understand certain aspects of yourself through language.

Basic Process

These exercises first lead you through metalinguistic play with everyday communication. Next you experiment with language as a tool that affects people's behavior, thinking, and values. Then you evaluate and transform some of your self-talk.

Exercise 1: Playing with Semantics through Poetry

Semantics is the study of meanings and connotations of words and symbols, including their meaning within the surrounding neighborhood of words.

   1. Read the following poem aloud a number of times:

> *I saw a man pursuing the horizon;*
> *Round and round they sped.*
> *I was disturbed at this;*
> *I accosted the man.*
> *"It is futile," I said,*
> *"You can never . . . "*
>
> *"You lie!" he cried,*
> *And ran on.*
>
> —Stephen Crane

2. Brainstorm at least five answers to the following questions: What are some things that people often pursue? What is your response to, comment about, or question to this pursuit? What would be the likely reaction of the other person to your response?

3. Reread the poem, substituting the words, phrases, or statements from your answers in the appropriate blanks in the poem below.

> *I saw a person pursuing _____;*
> *Round and round she sped.*
> *I was disturbed at this;*
> *I accosted the person.*
> *"_____," I said,*
> *"_____ ."*
>
> *"_____!" she cried,*
> *And ran on.*
>
> —Stephen Crane

4. Reflect by answering the following questions: What happened to the poem with each new substitution? Which substitutions did you like the most? Which were most surprising? Most revealing? Which substitutions brought about the most dramatic changes in the meaning of the poem? Which were unexpectedly profound? What have you learned about metalanguage?

Exercise 2: Playing with Syntax in Everyday Life

Syntax involves the rules that govern the order of words in speech or composition.

1. Play a game with the following sentences. The goal is to see how many different sentences you can make by rearranging the words. You may make slight grammatical alterations, for example, in person (he, she, him, her) or articles (a, an, the) if necessary, but the basic rule is that you must use all the words in each sentence in some form.

   ◆ **The husband only wanted to tell his wife about this.**

   ◆ **She decided to ask the new boy out for a date.**

   ◆ **The old man wanted to buy a present for his good friend.**

   ◆ **The young woman craved the fattening dessert the waiter described.**

   ◆ **As the president spoke, a titter spread across the crowd.**

2. Over the next several days, look for opportunities to play with syntax in things you read or in things you hear people say. How are certain words ordered to increase their impact on the listener or reader? How do meanings shift when word orders are changed? How do meanings shift when the context of hearing or reading is changed?

Exercise 3: Language as a Strategy to Move Others

1. Brainstorm words or phrases for each of the following categories: *Emotionally Charged Words/Phrases, Words/Phrases That Call for an Action/Response, Words/Phrases That Intimidate or Put Down,* and *Words/Phrases That Affirm, Support, Motivate.*

2. Over the next couple weeks, listen for the words and phrases people use, especially noting those you brainstormed.

3. At the end of the weeks, look over the chart and see if you notice any consistent word patterns; for example, maybe at school words challenge and call for action or response, whereas at home words affirm, support, and motivate.

4. For each situation, reflect on how it might be different if more words from the other categories were part of the typical verbal communication.

Exercise 4: Transforming Your Self-Talk through Affirmations*

1. List at least ten things in your life that please you a great deal. For each item on your list, make a note about what pleases you about that item and why you are glad it is in your life.

2. List at least ten things in your life that you do not like.

3. Transform each thing that you don't like into something that you like. List these transformations.

4. Burn the "Things in My Life That I Do Not Like" list.

5. Look over the "Transformations" list. Choose one item that you find especially interesting or pressing. Create a statement that affirms this item, celebrates its potential, or claims the promise of its fruition.

6. On separate sheets of paper, write out a story, an essay, a poem, and a song about your affirmation. Give yourself plenty of time to come up with a product that is meaningful to you. (You do not need to complete these products in one sitting.)

7. Repeat the process with several different items on your list, beginning with the easier ones to affirm and moving to the more difficult ones when you're ready.

8. Reflect on the exercise by answering the following questions: What parts made the greatest impression? Which parts were most difficult? Most interesting? Most fun? What surprises you the most? Which affirmations seem most exciting? Which items seem immediately realizable? Which seem long-term? Which are you looking forward to experiencing? How can you continue to use this exercise? What other areas of your life would you like to explore using this exercise?

*Adapted from Lazear, David. 1991. *Seven Ways of Knowing: Teaching for Multiple Intelligences* (Palatine, Ill.: Skylight).

Developing Your Funny Bone

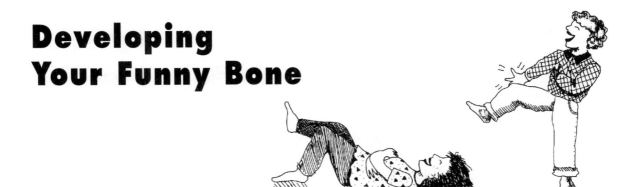

Did you hear the one about the guy who went into the bar . . . ?

> *Linguistic humor occurs with the classical pun, unexpected twists of the language, misunderstandings of the meanings of words, the earnest misuse of the language, and all the double meanings that run rampant in our communications.*

Playing with the English Language

Getting Started

The following exercises are most enjoyable with a group of at least eight to ten people. Recruit a group of friends and colleagues who would like to learn some new word games. You don't have to try all the exercises in one sitting or even with the same group of people. Give yourself plenty of time to get through all the exercises.

Basic Process

In the first exercise you'll have a chance to work on your pun-ability (guaranteed to produce many groans from your friends). The second exercise asks you to play with double meanings and potential misunderstanding of intended serious communication. In the third exercise you'll work on your capacity to come up with surprise endings.

Exercise 1: Developing Your Pun-Ability

1. With a partner, brainstorm a list of words and phrases that have potential double meanings, for example, *knight/night, please file that,* egg words (*yokes, scrambled, shells*), *shake before using, tear along dotted line.* Write your words and phrases on pieces of paper and put them in a hat.

2. Have each pair get together with another pair. Each pair draws three slips of paper from the other team's hat, then writes a dialogue that incorporates the words or phrases in a "punny" way, as in the following examples:
   "I'm serious!"
   "Pleased to meet you. I'm Roebuck!"

"I'm really in a jam!"
"Oh, that's too bad. Is it strawberry or grape?"

"You're really stupid for making that comment!"
"Well, if you think I'm stupid, you should see my brother. He's stooped way over like this!"

3. In round robin fashion, have each pair share its dialogue. (Groans and boos are acceptable, even encouraged! In fact, they may be an indicator of how successful the dialogue is.)

4. Ask people to keep lists of pun possibilities they encounter in their everyday lives and to share these next time you gather.

Exercise 2: Misunderstandings and Misuses of the Language

1. In his book *Anguished English*, Richard Lederer shares a wide variety of humorous misuses and misunderstandings of the English language:

> At a restaurant: Dinner Special—Turkey $2.35; Chicken or Beef $2.25; Children $2.00.

> Advertisement: Now is your chance to have your ears pierced and get an extra pair to take home.

> Highway sign: Drive slower when wet.

> Sign in store window: Why go elsewhere to be cheated when you can come in here?

> Newspaper headline: Defendant's speech ends in long sentence.

> Misspelling: On Thanksgiving we could smell the foul cooking.

2. Gather in teams of two or three. Come up with five items for each category that demonstrate similar misunderstandings and misuses of the language: newspaper headlines, road signs, advertisements, restaurant signs/menus, and interesting misspellings.

3. Have teams post their findings, then have a good time reading one another's lists.

4. Ask people to keep lists of other misuses and misunderstandings they encounter and to share them next time you gather.

Exercise 3: Unexpected Endings and Outcomes

1. Following are four miniexercises that explore linguistic humor through unexpected turns of events. Try one and ask the group if they would like to try others at another time.

Round Robin Storytelling

◆ On seven index cards write one of the following words per card: *Once, upon, a, time, there, was, a.* Keep the cards in order.

- Arrange the group in a circle. Starting with the tallest person in the circle and moving clockwise, give each person one of the cards.

- The tallest person reads her card and each person to the right reads his card in turn. Each person continues the story by adding one word at a time in turn.

- Continue around the circle at least seven times and see what happens to the story.

The Committee-Written Speech

- As a group, brainstorm a list of unusual and bizarre topics for a speech. Select one of the topics.

- On five index cards write the following, one per card: *Introduction, Point 1, Point 2, Point 3, Conclusion.* Fold the cards in half and place them in a hat.

- Divide the group into five—either partners or individuals, depending on the size of the group. Each pair (or individual) draws one of the cards from the hat.

- The pairs write their assigned parts of the speech without talking to the other pairs.

- When each pair has completed its writing, collect the five parts of the speech and choose one person to give the speech.

Can You Top This?

- Arrange the group in a circle. Ask for a volunteer to begin telling a tall tale with the starter, "I'm sure you'll find this difficult to believe, but last night I . . . "

- The person to her right says, "Oh, that's nothing! I can top that because last night I . . . "

- Continue around the circle with each person coming up with a more fantastic tale.

- After each person has told his tall tale, vote on the best one and, as a group, write a minidrama portraying the story.

Secret Essay Writing

- As a group, brainstorm a list of mundane topics for an essay.

- Select the most mundane topic from the list and imagine that the essay on this topic will be read to and critiqued by a group of Nobel Prize winners.

- The person wearing the brightest clothing writes the introductory sentence at the top of a piece of blank paper.

- He folds the top of the page down to hide the sentence. The person to his left writes what she thinks the next logical statement might be. She folds the paper so this sentence is hidden.

- Continue this process of writing, folding the paper, and passing the paper to the next person until the paper arrives at the last person in the circle. This person is to write a powerful and compelling conclusion.

- Pass the completed essay back to the first person, who reads the essay to the group.

2. After completing **each** miniexercise or game, lead the group in the following reflections: What words, phrases, and lines do you remember? What did you hear that was most surprising? What was most humorous? What was really bizarre or especially strange? What was most interesting about the process? What was most unexpected? What was fun? What was difficult? What happened to you as a group as you participated in the exercise? What did you learn about language-based humor from this experience? Brainstorm ways you could adapt this exercise to help you expand your creativity in daily verbal-linguistic communications with others.

The Sound and Rhythm of Language

"Hooked on Phonetics!" (how it sounds)

> *Have you ever been in a foreign country where you didn't understand the language but you could sense what was going on in a conversation just from the tone, pitch, and rhythmic patterns of others' speech? Sometimes our intuitions are accurate and sometimes, because of cultural differences, they are not. When we are operating in a familiar language, we can learn a great deal about another's true meanings when we tune in to the tonal and rhythmic patterns.*

The Tones and Rhythms of Speech

Getting Started

You need a tape recorder for exercise 1, which you can do alone. For exercise 2, you'll need a friend.

Basic Process

The first exercise focuses on the tonal aspects of speech, and the second deals with rhythmic patterns and vibrational qualities.

Exercise 1: Interpretive Reading and Speaking

1. Find a copy of the Declaration of Independence and read aloud the first part several times until you are comfortable with it.

2. Reread the passage aloud five times, and each time you read it, experiment with changing such things as what you emphasize, the tone of your voice, the pace of your reading, and so on. Notice how these subtle changes alter the meaning.

3. Read the passage into a tape recorder, trying to communicate the moods or emotions of the following situations: You are a great Shakespearean actor. You are very, very sleepy. You just learned that you won the lottery. You're reading to a baby lying in a crib. You're in the middle of the most terrifying scene in a terrifying movie. You've just finished eating your favorite dessert and it was fabulous. You are telling a hilarious joke. You are totally bored with what you have to say. You are an evangelist, trying to get people to commit their lives to this. You are a TV newscaster and this is your report of a typical news event on the evening news. You are delivering it as a keynote speech to a conference of stuffy academicians.

4. Play the tape for a trusted friend. Give her the list of situations. After each reading, stop the tape and ask this person to guess which situation you were trying to communicate. Ask for feedback.

5. Reflect on the exercise by answering the following questions: Which reading was most on target? Which did your partner feel was most on target? Which of the readings did you find most interesting? Most challenging? Which evoked things in you that you didn't know were there? What have you learned about the interpretive tonal and rhythmic aspects of verbal communication? Brainstorm at least five tonal or rhythmic strategies you want to incorporate consciously into your everyday communications.

Exercise 2: Secular Glossolalia

1. You need a partner for this exercise. Start by simply speaking to each other in gibberish. The rule in this game is that at no time are you to say or write anything that could be recognized as "real" language! Pretend that you are having a meaningful communication even though you are speaking nonsense.

2. As your gibberish continues, see if you can establish new "words" between you so that you will recognize them and know what is being talked about.

3. Next move into inventing descriptive words for the objects you have named, and try to use these new words to describe other things.

4. Reflect on the exercise by answering the following questions: What struck you? What do you remember? What did you find most intriguing? Most challenging? Most surprising? What was fun? What did you learn or discover about language?

Visual-Spatial Intelligence

Eidetic Images Practices

Basking in the Afterglow

> Eidetic images *are the "afterimages" you see when you have been staring at a bright light or candle or after a camera flashes. Sometimes you can still see the flash ten to fifteen minutes later! One way to strengthen your capacity to create vivid mental images is to work with these after images.*

Phase 1: Sensing Afterimages

Getting Started

For the first exercise, select a variety of objects with which to work, including a lighted candle, a burning lightbulb, and a bright metallic object. For the second exercise, select photographs, paintings, pictures, sculptures, or other objects that you find interesting—the more unusual the better. Choose items that have contrasting and bright colors; vivid images; a suggestion of movement; interesting shapes, patterns, and designs. Find a quiet, uncluttered space where you can work on the exercises—one in which you will not be disturbed or distracted while you are practicing.

Basic Process

The following exercises will help you develop the capacity to sense afterimages.

Exercise 1: Sensing the Afterimage (simple)

1. Place a burning candle on a flat surface in front of you. Close your eyes and spend a few minutes relaxing as fully as you can. Take several deep breaths and let go of any worries. Keep breathing deeply and bring yourself to the present, where you are aware only of yourself, your breathing, and your deep relaxation. Open your eyes and stare at the burning candle for a minute or so. Close your eyes and try to see the afterimage of the flame.

2. When you can no longer see the image, open your eyes and stare at the flame for another minute. Close your eyes and see how long you can see the after-image. Increase the length of time you see the afterimage each time.

3. Repeat the process with a burning lightbulb and the bright metallic object.

Exercise 2: Seeing the Afterimage (complex)

1. Select one of the objects and place it before you. Close your eyes and spend a few minutes relaxing as fully as you can. Take several deep breaths and let go of all worries. Keep breathing deeply and bring yourself to the present, where you are aware only of yourself, your breathing, and your deep relaxation.

2. Open your eyes and gaze intently, without blinking, at the photograph, painting, or object before you. When you must blink, close your eyes and try to continue to see (or imagine you are seeing) the object.

3. When you can no longer see or sense the presence of the object with your mind's eye, open your physical eyes and gaze intently at the object without blinking. When you must blink, close your eyes and try to sense the afterimage.

4. Continue this process, going back and forth between gazing intently at the object and closing your eyes and sensing the afterimage, until you feel that you have a strong inner sense of what you have been observing.

5. Repeat the process with other photographs, paintings, pictures, sculptures, or objects you have selected. Do exercise 2 until you achieve the strong inner sense of the afterimage.

6. Later in the day, when you need a break, pause and close your eyes and see if you can recall the afterimage from your earlier practice.

   The experience may range from a vague impression of the object to a hazy sight to a lingering inner sense to a full-blown reproduction. Continued work can help you strengthen your "inner seeing" capacities. This practice will also help you prepare for the imaging practices that follow.

Phase 2: Changing Afterimages

Getting Started

Use the same photographs, paintings, or other objects you used in phase 1. Choose one that you find particularly interesting. Find a quiet, relatively uncluttered space where you will not be disturbed.

Basic Process

Place the object in front of you in a way that you can give it your full attention and not be distracted. Shine a bright light on it so that you can vividly see its colors, shapes, textures, and patterns. Do the following exercises.

Exercise 1: Changing the Afterimage (simple)

1. Repeat the process you used in exercise 2 of the previous practice.

2. When you have achieved a strong inner sense of the selected object, begin to play with it in the following fashion: Open your eyes and stare at the object. Close your eyes and sense the afterimage. Imagine that a roaring lion suddenly appears in the scene you are picturing. Just as suddenly, the lion disappears. Open your eyes and gaze at the object. Close your eyes and sense the afterimage. Imagine that a raging fire has suddenly started in your scene. Just as suddenly it is gone. Open your eyes and gaze at the object. Close your eyes and sense the afterimage. Imagine that it has been suddenly transported to the bottom of the sea; imagine that it is on the Moon; transport it to a jungle setting.

Exercise 2: Changing the Afterimage (complex)

1. Repeat the process you used in exercise 2 of the previous practice.

2. When you have achieved a strong inner sense of the object, play with it. When your eyes are closed and you are sensing the afterimage, think of several other outrageous things to do with the image. Here are some suggestions to get you started: Imagine that everything in the afterimage is a brilliant orange (or other color). Imagine that an amazing display of fireworks is going off in the midst of your image. Imagine a variety of *extreme* weather conditions have just happened to your image. Imagine that a character from a movie has just shown up in your image. Imagine that your image is the backdrop for a TV advertisement. Imagine your entire family has just appeared in your image. Imagine that the president has suddenly appeared and is making a speech within your image. Imagine that a table filled with your favorite desserts is somewhere in your image.

3. Later in the day, when you need a break, pause, close your eyes, and see if you can recall the changed afterimage. During this break, see if you can play with the image, making additional changes, even when you don't have the object before you.

Graphic Representation Practices

Discovering the Latent Artist Within

> *Graphic representation uses the "external seeing" of the physical eyes and the ability to represent what we see. However, "artistic ability" or "talent" is not the issue in the following practices. They are concerned instead with intensifying our knowing capacities through the various media associated with the visual-spatial intelligence.*

Phase 1: Looking at an Art Form

Getting Started

Choose an art form such as photographs, paintings, sculptures, fabrics, videos, or anything that has a unique visual pattern (for example, tree bark, clouds, and so on).

Basic Process

Do the following process, question by question, reflecting on the art form you have chosen. Don't jump levels—the questions are designed to take you on a journey through different levels of visual-spatial cognitive processing. Each level is important for building your graphic representation capacities.

Spend a few minutes simply observing the art form you have chosen, then complete the following statements in a notebook or on a separate sheet of paper:

Objective Level (What in the art form immediately grabs your attention?)

To which part is your attention instantly drawn? What do you notice first? What colors strike you? What textures do you sense? What shapes, images, patterns, and designs jump out at you?

Affective Level (What are your feelings/emotional responses to the art form?)

If you could take something away from this art form what would you remove? What could you add to this art form? What feelings does this art form evoke in you?

Interpretive Level (What are some of the meanings you can see in the art form?)

What background music could you play for this art form? What does this art form remind you of or make you think about? What do you imagine is going on or has just happened?

Personal Level (What is your own relationship to and decision about the art form?)

What experiences in your own life do you identify with this art form or what does it call to mind? If you had to place this art form in your bedroom, where would you put it and why? If you had created this art form what would you have named it?

Phase 2: Creating a Montage

Getting Started

Gather a variety of magazines, preferably filled with many colorful pictures, images, patterns, and designs. You also need scissors, an 8 1/2-by-11-inch stiff backing sheet, and glue.

Basic Process

Decide the theme of your montage, then select images from the magazines that reflect your theme. Create your montage, then reflect on it.

Planning the Montage Focus

Brainstorm a list of three to five items for each category that follows: things I've been thinking about, things in the news that have caught my attention, and things that concern me in my school life.

Place a star beside one item from each list that is currently the most interesting or compelling. For each item you have selected, write a sentence that states the underlying concern or issue.

Reflect on your three sentences. Write the one sentence that represents a current priority. Write the one sentence that states an underlying common-theme. Write something perhaps unrelated to your sentences, that has emerged as an issue or concern. Choose a theme, issue, or concern you want to explore in your montage.

Creating the Montage

Your montage may directly or indirectly reflect the theme you have chosen. It may reflect insights, feelings, thoughts, associations, or profound knowings you have about the theme or a message you want to convey. (Follow the guidelines on page 115.)

- ◆ Look through the magazines you have gathered. When you find pictures that are related to the theme, tear them out. Trust your intuitions—don't get too analytical!

- When you have ten to fifteen pictures, cut out the specific images, patterns, or designs you want.

- Arrange the images on the backing paper. You don't have to use them all; you can always return to the magazines if you need more or different images. Allow this process to be intuitive, as if the images were arranging themselves.

- Do not glue anything in place yet, but play with the images, noting the impact they have in various arrangements. Ask yourself which arrangement is most appropriate to express the theme. Consider all aspects, including color, patterns, and designs.

- When you have an "Aha!" or "That's it!" sense about a particular arrangement, glue the pictures in place.

Reflecting on the Montage

Study the montage you have created and reflect on it by asking yourself the following questions: What particular images, pictures, patterns, designs, or colors immediately grab your attention? What surprises you? Shocks you? Delights you? Intrigues you? What experiences in your life does the montage call to mind? What title would you give it?

Montage Creation Guidelines

Following are some suggestions for creating a more powerful montage.

- The montage should be all pictures, patterns, images, and designs—no words—to increase the visual impact of the montage and its theme.

- Completely fill the backing paper with pictures, which prevents your attention being drawn to the blank space; you tend to see the montage as a whole.

- Use the colors of the pictures and the arrangement to enhance the feelings you wish to convey through the montage.

- Use only black-and-white pictures or color pictures, which helps maintain the focus of the montage and prevents it from becoming cluttered.

- Keep the pictures within the edges of the backing to frame the montage.

- Use the pictures and the arrangement to create a single impact on the viewer, one that is in line with the theme you have chosen.

Phase 3: Using an Art Form to Explore a Concern

Getting Started

Decide on the medium you will use and gather the necessary supplies. Find a quiet space where you will not be disturbed for about forty-five minutes. You need a large, uncluttered table or desk where you can lay out your supplies and have plenty of work space.

Basic Process

You choose a concern in your life and explore it in a variety of ways using the media of the visual-spatial intelligence.

The Art Form

1. List five to ten concerns you have about the future. Include concerns for your family, friends, school, and personal life.

2. Choose one of the concerns you would like to explore and write several sentences about it: What are some of the different aspects of the concern? How does it make you feel? Why is this a concern for you? What are the questions or issues it poses for you?

3. With your eyes closed, try to imagine the following as they relate to your concern: What colors do you associate with it? What shapes? What textures? Smells? Tastes? If the concern were a weather condition, what would it be? What kind of background music does this concern need? If the concern were an animal, what would it be? What objects do you associate with the concern? What persons do you associate with it? What places? What times?

4. When you are ready and you feel you have a strong inner sense of the concern, open your eyes. Using the specific visual medium you have chosen, create a visual representation of your concern. Use the various images and associations you made with the concern to guide you as you create your art form.

5. Give yourself plenty of time. Allow things to happen naturally and intuitively. Create whatever comes to you in the moment. Your creation may take a variety of forms, including an abstract representation, something highly symbolic, a literal representation, a creation that helps you express something for yourself, or one that expresses something about the concern to someone else.

Reflect on this exercise by responding to the following questions while you study the art form closely: What immediately grabs your attention? What shapes do you see? What colors? What patterns? What designs? What surprises you? What delights you? What intrigues you? What obvious connections do you see between the art form and your initial concern? What less obvious or symbolic connections do you see between the art form and your initial concern? What do you see that may help you deal more adequately with the concern? If the art form had a voice, what would it say? What title would you give it? Find an appropriate place in your home or classroom to display your art—a place where you will see it often. Continue to explore the art form over the next couple of weeks and see what else it may reveal to you and what else you discover about it.

Intelligence Builders for Every Student © 1998 Zephyr Press, Tucson, AZ

Visualization Practices

Seeing with the Mind's Eye

> *Visualizing is the mind's natural (and probably first) way of thinking. Experiment with each different type and reflect on what happens when you do the exercises.*
>
> *Each person has a unique experience. Some literally see what is suggested—even in 3-D and technicolor with stereophonic sound. Others see as if through a thick fog. Some may have only a vague impression or sense of what has been suggested. There is no right or wrong experience.*
>
> *If you wish, you can trick your brain into seeing more vividly by simply relaxing, not trying too hard, and saying to yourself, "Okay, I'm not literally seeing what is being suggested, but I'm going to pretend I'm seeing it!" Or "Okay, I'm not seeing it, but if I were, what would I be seeing?"*

Planning Effective Visualization Experiences

Visualization Creation Work Sheet Process

Review the types of visualizations on pages 121–122. The Visualization Planning Work Sheet on page 123 gives you a step-by-step format for designing effective visualization exercises. Thinking through each stage ensures that the exercise you create is compatible with the way the brain works. Refer to the process column while you fill out the application column. See if you can identify in the practice exercises already presented the various stages listed on the work sheet. Note the wide variety of ways these four stages were employed.

The Preparation

Taking time to prepare yourself adequately for a visualization is key to making the process work. Part of your task is to identify the problem, question, challenge, or situation that is to be the focus of the exercise. Don't worry—this task does not limit you. Rather it helps you focus creative energy on finding new options or solutions.

> *In the third column of the work sheet write a couple of sentences stating the focus of the exercise you are designing, as well as the type of visualization you feel is most appropriate.*

VISUALIZATION TYPE	WHEN TO USE IT	PRACTICE EXERCISES
Open Screen *Open screen visualization exercises help you become aware of your inner network of images, feelings, reflections, and associations related to a topic.*	■ when you are trying to sort through concerns or issues ■ when you need to brainstorm options for a decision you are facing ■ when you want to expand on or further explore an idea ■ when you want to have fun or to see what your mind will produce on a topic	1. Decide the focus of the exercise. 2. Imagine yourself relaxing in a large, comfortable chair in your ideal room. 3. Pretend there is a state-of-the-art, large-screen TV in the room. Turn it on. Flip the channels until you find the program that is about your focus. 4. As you watch the program, be as aware as you can of everything you are seeing, feeling, sensing, and thinking about. 5. When you have seen enough, turn off the TV and spend a few minutes reflecting on what you experienced. 6. Imagine yourself leaving the room and coming back to your everyday situation.
Inner Guide *Inner guide visualization helps you tap into the mind's natural creativity to solve problems and gain insight into a particular concern.*	■ when you have a difficult problem you are trying to solve and feel you need some help thinking things through ■ when you have made a decision about a difficult issue and want to evaluate the pros and cons of the decision ■ when you are facing a challenge you're not sure how to meet and you need some encouragement and advice ■ when you have to make a decision about something that involves a number of complex issues and you need to explore some of your options	1. Choose the concern you want to explore. 2. Pretend you are strolling along a path that winds through a beautiful, peaceful wooded area or a forest. It is a warm spring day. 3. Your journey eventually leads to a clearing where you find a very wise teacher. What does she look like? 4. Imagine yourself having a conversation with this teacher, asking questions related to your concern. After each question, pause and listen to what the teacher says or does (the response may be nonverbal). 5. If you wish, you may want to have paper and pencil nearby to record the responses of this wise teacher. 6. When you feel the conversation has come to a natural stopping place, thank the teacher for the advice and imagine yourself on the path, which will take you out of the woods and back to your everyday life. 7. Spend a few minutes reflecting on the conversation you had with the wise teacher, evaluating the answers given to your questions.

Intelligence Builders for Every Student © 1998 Zephyr Press, Tucson, AZ

VISUALIZATION TYPE	WHEN TO USE IT	PRACTICE EXERCISES
Creativity Tapping *Creativity tapping visualization helps you maximize your natural creative process and makes your creative intuitions work better.*	• when you are looking for a fresh approach to a mundane task • when you are stuck in any kind of routine or habitual behavior that you want to break out of • when you want to explore a new range of creative options for a project you are working on • when you are bored and want to get a new perspective on life	1. Decide the focus of the exercise. 2. Get into a relaxed and comfortable position and close your eyes. Take ten deep breaths, using the exhalation to help you relax fully. 3. Imagine you are slowly ascending a spiral staircase that has three levels. Each level has a different gallery for you to explore: ▶ The first level is the gallery of the current situation (here you see the details and issues related to your concern). ▶ The second level is the gallery of past efforts (here you see all the things you have already tried). ▶ The third level is the gallery of wild new possibilities (here you see things that you have never considered or tried). 4. Pretend that you are walking through the three galleries, beginning with the current situation gallery. When you have thoroughly explored its contents, move to the gallery on the next level, then the next. 5. After you have explored the third gallery you discover there is one more level and one more gallery called the gallery of creative resolve. The gallery is empty except for a desk and chair. 6. Imagine yourself sitting at the desk. Take a blank sheet of paper and list relevant ideas you have seen, discoveries you have made, and intuitions you have sensed from your visit to the galleries of the spiral staircase. 7. When you are finished, close your eyes and imagine yourself slowly descending the spiral staircase, passing through the different galleries. 8. When you arrive at the ground floor, open your eyes and read the list of ideas you gleaned from your journey.

VISUALIZATION TYPE	WHEN TO USE IT	PRACTICE EXERCISES
Patterns of Connection *Patterns of connection visualization helps you establish a relationship between your everyday life and the larger story and patterns of which you are a part.*	■ when you are feeling confused about and/or are questioning the meaning and purpose of your life ■ when you are trying to understand the significance of an everyday occurrence in the larger scheme of things ■ when you are trying to help someone else with a problem or concern he is facing ■ when you feel the need to re-establish a link between your "local self" and a more global or comprehensive view of reality	1. Decide the concern of the exercise. 2. Select an object from nature or a pictorial representation of such an object (for example, a great tree, an interesting rock, a plant in full bloom, flowing water). 3. Spend time getting into a deep state of relaxation. 4. Gaze intently at the object, noticing the various shapes, colors, and patterns you see. 5. What do these patterns/shapes/colors remind you of? What do you associate with them? 6. Close your eyes and visualize vividly the concern of this exercise. 7. Open your eyes and look at the object before you. Where do you see shapes, patterns, images, and colors that are connected to or similar to those of your concern? 8. Pretend this object can speak to you about your concern. What is it saying? What is its message? How would the object deal with your concern?
Symbolic/ Mythic Journeys *Symbolic/mythic journey visualization helps you explore the unconscious mythic images and symbols that are part of your self-understanding.*	■ when you sense the need for a deeper or archetypal perspective on something with which you are struggling ■ when you are especially intrigued with and want to know more about any character you have encountered in a novel, story, movie, or play ■ when you have been deeply moved by an archetypal image from your spiritual practice ■ when you have been deeply moved by a so-called ordinary everyday experience and you suspect that there is a deeper significance in this experience	1. Decide the focus of the exercise. Choose a fictional or mythic character you feel might have some relationship to or insight about this concern. 2. Briefly recall everything you currently know or associate with this character. 3. Do a relaxation process. 4. Visualize yourself in a typical situation where the focus you decided earlier is clearly manifest. 5. Pretend the character walks into this situation and takes your place. 6. Imagine that you are watching a movie of how this character handles your life. What does the character do? What are the character's feelings and thoughts? What decisions does the character make? Are they similar or dissimilar to your own? 7. Record your reflections on what you learned by watching this character living your life and dealing with your issues.

VISUALIZATION TYPE	WHEN TO USE IT	PRACTICE EXERCISES
Past and Future Journeys *Past and future visualizations help you harvest learnings, insights, and reflections from the past and anticipate learnings, insights, and reflections in your future.*	■ when you are trying to recapture wisdom or insights from a previous stage of your life or from a previous period of history ■ when you are struggling with the potential impact of current decisions on your future life ■ when you need to remember or call upon learnings, discoveries, or insights from the past ■ when you feel as though you need a crystal ball to anticipate what the future might bring	1. Decide the focus of the exercise. 2. Lie down on the floor or some other comfortable place. Close your eyes and take several deep breaths to help you relax and let go of worries and concerns. 3. Imagine that you are getting lighter and lighter by the minute, until you are so light that you are able to float. 4. Imagine that you have floated up out of the room where you started and that you are slowly heading into the clouds. 5. From this vantage point you can see the whole past and the whole future. Visualize the focus of the exercise. Do you need to journey into the past, the future, or both to seek answers? 6. When you arrive at your destination, slowly float down into the midst of the situation you have envisioned. Articulate the issue or concern for which you are seeking wisdom or insight. 7. Wait, in a state of passive expectation, paying attention to everything that happens in your active imagination. 8. When you have seen enough, allow yourself to float into the clouds and return to the room whence you began your journey. 9. Open your eyes, stretch, and sit up. Take out paper and pencil, and record what you have known, sensed, and discovered in this journey as it relates to your initial concern.

The Relaxation

A key factor in tapping the mind's natural capacities to form mental images is to relax the body, for the body is both the guardian of and pathway to the unconscious realms of the human psyche. Your goal is to relax the body so no tension remains, relax the emotions so that feelings of calm dominate, and relax the mind so that all concerns are temporarily put aside. You are trying get into a state of passive receptiveness, abandoning the tendency to be analytical and evaluative. You are getting ready to "go with the flow" of the process of imaginistic thinking, as when you are daydreaming.

> *In the third column of the work sheet, outline the relaxation process you use in the exercise, for example, progressive relaxation from the toes up to the head; tensing the body, then suddenly releasing the tension several times; lying on the floor or a sofa and imagining that you are floating.*

The Journey

The journey is the heart of the exercise. There are several important parts:

1. Devise a mental gimmick to achieve a state of passive awareness where you watch the process of the exercise, almost as an outside observer.

2. Create a central image to move the focus from the everyday world to a state of introspection, insight, inspiration, and revelation.

3. Work with the central image in a way that helps you make connections with the issue you are addressing.

4. Allow plenty of time for the inner seeing process to occur (realizing that "real time" and "subjective time" are not the same because in the inner world things tend to happen more quickly and often at greater levels of complexity).

> *In the third column of the work sheet list the step-by-step procedures you use to facilitate the visualization process, including the mental gimmick, the central image for the journey, and the way you work with it in relation to the focus during the journey.*

The Reflection

In many ways, this part of the visualization exercise is the most important, for this is where you return from the journey and harvest the insights, discoveries, and wisdom. This part is also when you acknowledge the value of, express gratitude for, and resolve to pay more attention to this important inner seeing dimension of the self. Just as with the external dimensions of the self, it is important to nurture the continued development and strengthening of this aspect of the mind.

> *In the third column of the work sheet list your plan for recording the insights, discoveries, feelings, possible answers, and new options received during the process of the exercise.*

Visualization Planning Work Sheet

Planning Effective Imaging Experiences

Stage	Process	Particular Application
Preparation	**Discern the focus of the exercise:** ■ What concern/issue do you want to explore? ■ What questions? ■ What are you seeking?	
Relaxation	**Prepare the mind and body for the exercise:** ■ Find a quiet place. ■ Find a comfortable position. ■ Use a technique to relax the mind.	
The Journey	**Exercise steps:** ■ Move your thinking and awareness to a state of introspection, self-reflection/awareness, insight, or discovery. ■ Pretend you are an objective witness, simply watching and being aware of what is occurring. ■ Create a central image for the journey, deepen it, expand it, play with it. ■ Allow plenty of time for the inner process of the visualization to occur.	
The Reflection	**Debrief yourself:** ■ Record your feelings, insights, reflections, discoveries, thoughts. ■ Express your gratitude for the experience and promise yourself to try it again.	

Mind Mapping Practices

A Picture Is Worth a Thousand Words

> *Mind mapping, invented by Tony Buzan and described in his book* Use Both Sides of the Brain, *is an easy and enjoyable way to make meaningful use of images, patterns, designs, and colors that are part of everyday life. A mind map is a visual web that gets you to think and write in shapes and symbols. Usually a mind map starts with an image of a central idea, and associated images branch off from it. Mind maps can be simple or complex.*

The Basic Mind Mapping Process

Mind mapping is a wonderful, practical tool that helps you strengthen your natural visual-spatial capabilities. Following are fifteen suggestions to help you create your own mind maps.

1. Gather your supplies ahead of time: a blank sheet of unlined paper and a variety of colored marking pens. Clear a space on a table or desk so you have plenty of room to work, and sit in a comfortable chair.

2. Start in the center of the page with the topic and a symbolic representation of it.

3. Work outward in all directions, making branches from the topic idea. Create patterns, symbols, colors, and images that reflect your unique associations with the central idea.

4. Look for well-defined clusters and sub-clusters of items, keeping to five to seven groupings.

5. Use key words and phrases to help you remember the associations you have symbolized in your drawings.

6. Use color and 3-D perspectives in your symbols.

7. Print, rather than write, your words for more distinct and memorable images.

8. Put the words on the line, not at the ends of the lines.

9. Use only one word or short phrase per line.

10. Make the patterns, colors, and images noteworthy, even odd. The mind will remember them better.

11. Use arrows, colors, designs, and so on to show connections among parts of the mind map.

12. Use personal codes for fun and effectiveness.

13. Build the mind map quickly. The more spontaneous it is, the better you capture associations as they occur to you.

14. Be creative and original.

15. Have fun.

Mind Mapping a Familiar Activity

Getting Started

Brainstorm a list of activities such as hobbies, sports, outings, and everyday tasks you perform and know well. Select one of these as the focus of your mind map.

Basic Process

1. **Name the focus activity and draw it.** Write the name of the focus activity in the center of your paper and draw an image that symbolizes the activity (for example, a football, a stove, a bicycle, a musical instrument).

2. **Name aspects and associations and draw them.** What are the various aspects of this activity or things you associate with it? For each one you think of, draw a branch off of the central image. Label the branches and draw any images that visually symbolize these aspects and associations.

3. **Name relationships and draw them.** Look for connections among the associations you have drawn and draw lines that link these. Write words or short phrases that name the relationships and draw images that visually communicate these connections.

4. **Reflect on your completed mind map.** Spend a few minutes looking at your mind map and appreciating your creative work. Pretend you are using it as a visual aid to help someone else understand your focus activity. How would you walk them through your mind map? What would you say to explain the parts?

Mind Mapping a To-Do List

Getting Started

Brainstorm a list of things that you need to remember to do during the coming week or day (for example, studying for a test, people you need to call, or tasks you want to accomplish).

Basic Process

1. **Draw the central image.** Visually represent your list in the center of the page. Include the current date as part of your central image.

2. **Draw the specific to-do's.** Read over your list and draw a branch for each item. On each branch make a visual representation to remind you of each item. Remember, no words!

3. **Look for relationships.** Look for links between the images you have drawn, and draw lines to connect these items. Then draw images that visually communicate the relationships you have seen. No words!

4. **Reflect on your completed mind map.** Don't throw away your written to-do list, but store it in an accessible place. During the week, try to rely only on your mind map to help you stay on course. At the end of the week, reflect: How has the mind map been helpful? How would you do it differently next time?

Mind Mapping a Lecture

Getting Started

Write the title or focus of the lecture in the center of the page. Begin as you did before, but this time you may integrate words and phrases (as long as you keep them to a minimum!).

Basic Process

1. **Draw a central image.** Write the title, topic, or focus of the meeting or lecture in the center of the page and draw an image you associate with it.

2. **Draw images of anticipated points.** During the introduction, see if you can discern the points the speaker plans to address (or items that will be discussed in a meeting). For each one, draw a branch from the central image. Write a word or phrase and draw a simple image that you associate with it.

3. **Visually capture the ideas.** As the speaker talks or participants express their ideas, draw additional branches off of the original branches. Limit yourself to one or two words on the lines and include images to capture what is being said. As you listen, draw connections between associated points.

4. **Reflect on your completed mind map.** What stands out? What feelings and ideas does the map express or evoke? What were the most important parts of the lecture or meeting for you? What changes in the process do you want to make next time?

Mind Mapping a Problem or Concern

Getting Started

Begin by writing several lines that state as clearly and completely as you can the problem, issue, concern, or challenge you wish to explore in your mind map.

Basic Process

1. **Draw a central image.** In the center of the page draw a pattern, shape, design, or picture of the issue, including any words or phrases needed to more fully express the concern.

2. **Draw related images.** Think about the various aspects of the issue, and for each aspect, draw a branch from the central image, label the branch, and create an image that visually symbolizes it for you.

3. **Visually brainstorm.** For each "aspect branch," brainstorm possible ideas and solutions on branches. Label each new branch and create additional images that symbolize these ideas for you. (**Note:** Don't filter out anything you think of. Simply add it to your mind map. You can evaluate your ideas later.)

4. **Look for connections.** Now look at your mind map. Do you see any common images? Do you see any connections among your ideas? If so, draw these connections on your map.

5. **Reflect on your completed mind map.** Ask yourself, "What do these connections and images reveal about the possible solutions to the problem?" Reflect: "How has my mind map given me a new perspective? Next time I mind map an issue, how do I want to change the process?"

Visual Puzzles Practices

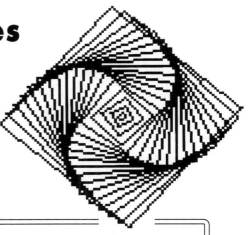

It's All a Matter of Perspective

In this section we are concerned with fine-tuning our external seeing, or seeing with our physical eyes. Often something we think we understand seems totally different when viewed in a different way. Just consider viewing a city skyline from the ground versus from an airplane. Or consider optical illusions, such as the popular picture of the beautiful young woman that can also be seen as an old woman or the two faces gazing at each other that can also be perceived as a vase.

Finding Visual Patterns

Getting Started

Begin with an exercise you find intriguing, then go on to work with the others until you have solved them all. However, don't stop with the exercises presented here. Move beyond these to some of the many visual puzzles and games that are widely available.

Basic Process

Each exercise that follows involves simply seeing "what is there" with your physical eyes. The exercises are designed to help you fine-tune your external vision capacities.

Exercise 1: What's Different in These Pictures?

1. In the children's section of your favorite bookstore, find a book that has differences puzzles. Work with them until you can quickly and easily see the differences.

2. Create some of your own pictures (for example, through photography, pattern drawings, magazine montages) and try them on your friends.

Exercise 2: Finding Your Way through a Maze

1. In your favorite bookstore, find a book of mazes. Find your way through the same maze twice, starting once from each end.

2. Create mazes of your own and see if you can get some of your friends to solve them.

Exercise 3: Connect-the-Dots Pictures

1. Get a workbook of connect-the-dots pictures and see how quickly you can learn to discern what they are.

2. Make some connect-the-dots pictures by laying thin pieces of paper over pictures and making connecting dot patterns that would more or less reproduce the pictures. Have others work them.

Gestalt Shifts

Getting Started

Gestalt is a German word that translates as "worldview" or "perspective." As with the last practice, begin with the exercise you find most intriguing and work with the others until you have solved all the puzzles. These puzzles are simply an introduction. Find additional resources and try some others that are more complex.

Basic Process

Each exercise that follows involves seeing "what is there" by playing with your vision and shifting your perception at will.

Exercise 1: Optical Illusions (simple)

1. Look at the following pictures and practice shifting your perspective back and forth according to what is suggested under each picture.

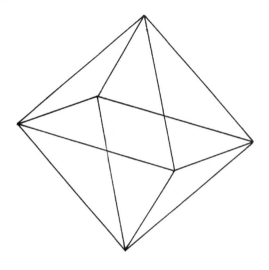

Gaze at the three-dimensional octahedron. See if you can get the various planes to change places (that is, see a top view, a bottom view, a front-to-back view, and so on).

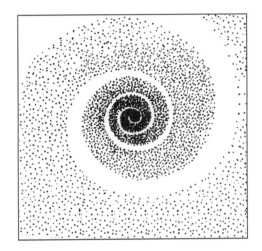

Gaze intently at the spiral; See if you can create a visual sense of movement in the pattern. Make it stand still, then move once again. (Hint: Squint your eyes to blur the box.)

Gaze at the design without blinking your eyes until you get a pulsing sensation in the picture.

Can you make this picture be first a rabbit, then a duck? (Hint: Rotate the picture.)

Exercise 2: Finding "Hidden" Images (simple)

1. If your newspaper carries "Find Waldo," clip out the feature every week for three or four months and do the exercise; that is, keep hunting until you find Waldo. At the end of three or four months, go back to the first picture and work your way through the collection again. Has your ability to find Waldo improved?

Exercise 3: Finding "Hidden" Images (complex)

Buy a *Magic Eye* book or borrow one. Learn how to look at the various patterns presented in the pictures so that you can see the hidden images. Work with the following techniques until you see the 3-D image in the pattern.

*   ◆ Place two small "sticky dots" (of the same color) at the top center of the picture. Stare at the dots intently (that is, without blinking) until they converge and appear to be one dot. Continue to focus on the converged dot, drop your gaze slightly to the picture below, and see if you can see the image.

*   ◆ Pretend that the picture is a window and that you are looking through it. Don't look at the picture—look beyond it. Keep gazing beyond it and see if the 3-D image emerges for you.

*   ◆ Cover the picture with a blank transparency or a piece of cellophane. Look for and concentrate on your own reflection in the cellophane. When you clearly see your own reflection, allow your peripheral vision to see the 3-D image.

Spatial Intelligence Practices

Isn't that Spatial!?!

> *Spatial capacities involve such things as the ability to transfer symbolic spatial information to its concrete spatial component (for example, using landmarks to find directions, reading a map, or connecting your new CD player or VCR to your stereo system or TV); developing spatial sensitivity and following spatial directions (for example, knowing where you are and finding your way around an area); and understanding spatial relationships and being able to act accurately upon such knowledge (for example, parallel parking).*

> *The exercises in this section are in sequence, and they are designed to develop your spatial intelligence. Therefore, start with the first exercise and work at it until you have mastered it, then move to the next. Most of the exercises require you to work with another person. This person need not understand as much about multiple intelligences as you do, but she should be someone you trust and with whom you are comfortable.*

Visual Clues to Spatial Reality

Getting Started

For these two exercises you need a trusted person. Begin with exercise 1 and do it until you have achieved a comfortable level of success, then move to the second exercise.

Basic Process

The following exercises involve a simple, or warm-up, level and a complex level. The complex exercises are at the heart of the spatial skills we are trying to build.

Exercise 1: Scavenger Hunt: Landmarks (simple)

1. Ask your partner to hide an object you have both chosen. He creates a set of written instructions to lead you to the object. The instructions focus on landmarks. Have your partner put the instructions in a sealed envelope.

2. Later, when your partner is not present, open the instructions and see if you can follow them to find the object. After you have found the object, meet with your partner and reflect on your experience.

3. Repeat the process, only this time ask your partner to record the instructions on an audiocassette tape, focusing on landmarks.

4. Later, when your partner is not present, listen to the tape (several times if necessary). See if you can find the object, relying on your memory of the landmarks. Meet after you have found the object and reflect on your experience. Note the similarities and differences between using the written instructions and the tape. Which was easier for you?

Exercise 2: Scavenger Hunt: Map Reading (complex)

1. Ask your partner to hide an object you have both chosen. She creates a map and marks where the object is hidden with an X. The map itself should have *no words*. However, your partner may create a legend that has a *few* words to explain the visual symbols. Your partner puts the map in a sealed envelope.

2. Later, when your partner is not present, open the envelope and see if you can read the map to find the object. After you have found the object, meet with your partner and reflect on your experience.

3. Ask your partner to create a map of a secret place, marking the location with an X. The map itself should have *no words* except for a legend to explain the visual symbols.

4. With your partner present, see if you can follow the map and take your partner to the secret place. Your partner gives no verbal or nonverbal clues until you think you have arrived at the secret place. She will say yes if you are right, no if you are wrong. If the answer is no, try again, relying only on the map.

5. After you have arrived at the secret place, reflect on your experience.

Spatial Sensitivity

Getting Started

These exercises require you to work with a partner. Choose someone you trust. If your partner is willing, you could switch roles on each exercise so that half the time you are the guide, but do not make switching a requirement.

Basic Process

The exercises deal with developing your spatial location sensing capacities (even when you are not looking!) and on developing your capacities for knowing spatial directions. Get warmed up with the simple exercise and move on to the complex.

Exercise 1: Blind Walk (simple)

1. Begin at your front door and take a walking tour of your entire home, carefully observing where the furniture is positioned, where various objects are, which parts of the floor are covered with carpets or rugs, and where the doorways are.

2. Return to the front door. Ask your partner to blindfold you. Repeat the walking tour, accompanied by your partner, who is your safety guide, speaking or touching you only to prevent you from damaging something or hurting yourself. As you walk, talk about what you are experiencing.

3. When you have reached the end of your tour ask your guide to select things in various rooms for you to find while blindfolded (for example, find the telephone, go turn the TV on, find your toothbrush). This process is an opportunity to exercise your spatial sense of your home.

4. Find your way to your favorite chair and remove the blindfold. Spend some time reflecting on your experience. Share what happened to you as you did it, and ask your partner to share observations, including suggestions of strategies you could employ to improve your performance.

5. Thank your partner for helping you, and if she wishes, reverse the roles.

Exercise 2: Blind Walk (complex)

1. Ask your partner to be your guide and go together to an interesting outdoor space that you know fairly well. Together walk around the space, familiarizing yourself with it (for example, notice where various objects and landmarks are, note the grade of the land, texture of the terrain).

2. Have your guide blindfold you. Hold his arm or hand and ask him to lead you around this space taking the same route you traveled before. Your partner acts as your safety guide to prevent you from hurting yourself.

3. As you walk, talk about what you are experiencing and where you think you are. If your sense is incorrect, the guide may tell you where you are.

4. When you have returned to the beginning point, ask your guide to take you on another walk, this time trying to get you lost. When you stop, see if you can tell your partner where you are. He may tell you that you are correct or where he has taken you. Try this exercise again and again, each time guessing where you are, until you feel you have a blind sense of the location.

5. Reflect on your experience. Share what happened to you and ask your partner to say what he observed and to suggest strategies you could employ to improve your performance.

6. Thank your partner for helping you, and if he agrees, reverse roles.

Understanding Spatial Relationships

Getting Started

You need to gather some special objects to perform the exercises in this section. Read the following procedures and gather the necessary props. Start with the exercise you find most intriguing.

Basic Process

The first exercise involves your bodily-kinesthetic as well as spatial intelligence. The second works with a more abstract process of seeing and understanding relationships between objects in space.

Exercise 1: Sink the Paper in the Basket

1. Wad fifteen to twenty pieces of scrap paper. Place an empty wastebasket about three feet in front of your chair and place the wads of paper at your side.

2. One by one, toss the paper wads into the wastebasket. After you have tossed all the wads in, move the wastebasket two feet farther away and repeat the process until you succeed again.

3. Move the wastebasket two feet farther away and repeat the process. Continue until you achieve the same success as when the wastebasket was at five feet.

4. Continue the process until the wastebasket is about ten feet from your chair. Toss until all wads go in.

Exercise 2: Playing Checkers with a Formidable Foe

1. Set up a checkerboard for a game. You will play this game of checkers against yourself!

2. Proceed as if there were another person sitting on the opposite side of the board. Make your first move. Then move around the table to the other position and make your first move. Continue this process in a fairly rapid, intuitive fashion, each time trying to outsmart the "other player," until each player has made seven to ten moves.

3. Stop and analyze the spatial relationships you see on the board. Ask yourself the following questions: Which player seems to be in the best position? What leads you to this conclusion? What seems to be the strategy of each player? As you observe the relationships among the checker pieces, what moves put each player in a better position?

4. Return to the game and try to implement the moves that maintain one player's advantage and also help the other player gain the advantage. Play out four of five more moves, proceeding in a relatively rapid, intuitive fashion, just as if you were playing against each opponent.

5. Stop and analyze the new relationships among the checker pieces you see on the board. Ask yourself the following questions: What has changed? Which of the players now has the advantage? What leads you to this conclusion? At this point what strategy would help each player gain the advantage over the other?

6. Return to the game and try to implement the distinct strategies you have conceived for each player. Play out the game until one player wins.

7. Shake hands with yourself, congratulating the victor and commiserating with the loser. Reflect on the process of the game: What struck you as you played this game against yourself? Which player were you most in tune with? Why or in what ways? What about understanding spatial relationships did you learn from each player? (Make a list of these learnings.) How can you apply these learnings to everyday life in situations where you need to understand spatial relationships?

Appendix

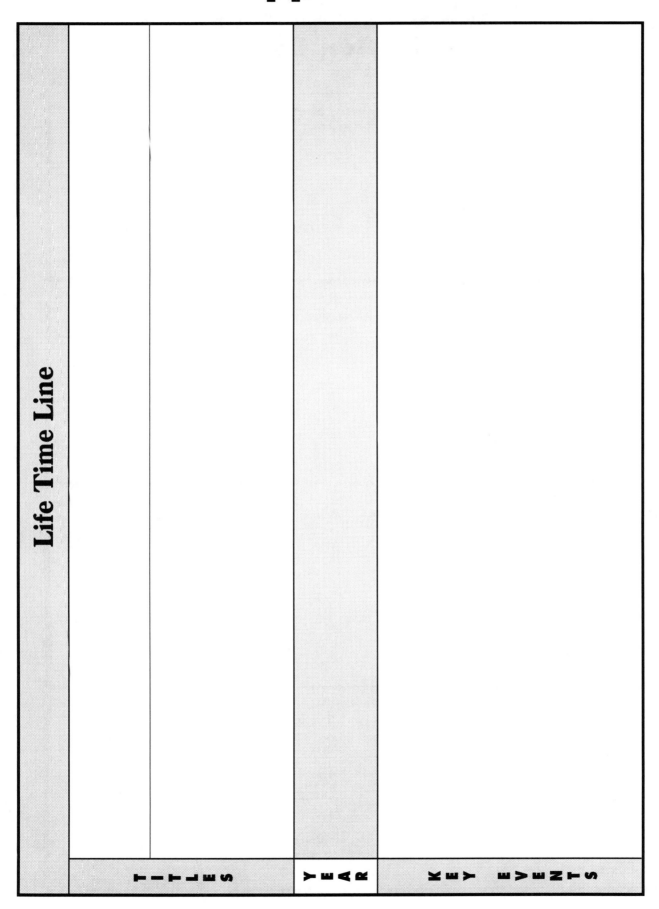

Life Time Line

TITLES | YEAR | KEY EVENTS

Intelligence-Building
Reflection Log

What were my major discoveries about this intelligence?

What role does this intelligence play in my daily life?

What do I need to do to keep this intelligence alive and growing?

The next steps for me and this intelligence are

Multiple Intelligences Bibliography

Armstrong, T. 1993. *Seven Kinds of Smart: Identifying and Developing Your Many Intelligences*. New York: Penguin.

———. 1994. *Multiple Intelligences in the Classroom*. Alexandria, Va.: ASCD.

Campbell, B. 1994. *Multiple Intelligence Handbook*. Stanwood, Wash.: Campbell.

Campbell, L., B. Campbell, and D. Dickinson. 1992. *Teaching and Learning through Multiple Intelligences*. Seattle: New Horizons for Learning.

Common Miracles: The New American Revolution in Learning. 1993. Video. New York: ABC News.

Feuerstein, R. 1980. *Instrumental Enrichment*. Baltimore, Md.: University Park Press.

Gardner, H. 1985. *Frames of Mind*. New York: Basic.

———. 1991a. *Multiple Intelligences: The Theory in Practice*. New York: Basic.

———. 1991b. *The Unschooled Mind: How Children Think and How Schools Should Teach*. New York: Basic.

———. 1994. *Creating Minds: An Anatomy of Creativity Seen through the Lives of Freud, Einstein, Picasso, Stravinsky, Eliot, Graham, and Gandhi*. New York: Basic.

Houston, J. 1982. *The Possible Human*. Los Angeles: J.P. Tarcher.

Jensen, E. 1995. *Brain-Based Teaching and Learning*. Del Mar, Calif.: Turning Point.

Lazear, D. 1998. *Eight Ways of Knowing: Teaching for Multiple Intelligences*. Palatine, Ill.: Skylight.

———. 1999. *Pathways of Learning: Teaching Students and Parents about Multiple Intelligences*. Tucson, Ariz.: Zephyr Press.

———. 1998. *Multiple Intelligence Approaches to Assessment: Solving the Assessment Conundrum*. rev. ed. Tucson, Ariz.: Zephyr Press.

Machado, L. A. 1980. *The Right to Be Intelligent*. New York: Pergamon.

Sternberg, R. G. 1984. *Beyond I.Q.: A Triarchic Theory of Human Intelligence*. New York: Cambridge University Press.

Sylwester, R. 1995. *A Celebration of Neurons: An Educator's Guide to the Human Brain*. Alexandria, Va.: ASCD.

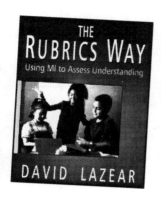

TAP YOUR MULTIPLE INTELLIGENCES

Posters for the Classroom

text by David Lazear

illustrations by Nancy Margulies

Grades 3–12

This handy set of 8 colorful posters will remind your students to use all of their intelligences. Includes the naturalist!

8 full-color, 11" x 17" posters.
1811-J . . . $27

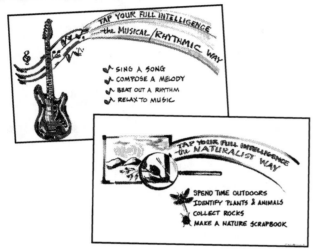

STEP BEYOND YOUR LIMITS

Expanding Your MI Capacities

by David Lazear

Professional Development

Gain valuable insights and nurture your intelligences with a powerful learning tool designed for your development. Each tape has an accompanying workbook that leads you on a self-guided, step-by-step, capacity-building and enhancement program. The workbooks contain carefully designed exercises for each intelligence.

Eight 40-minute audiotapes and 7 workbooks: One tape on each intelligence and one overview tape; one workbook for each intelligence..
1914-J . . . $175

ORDER FORM

Qty.	Item #	Title	Unit Price	Total
	1092-J	The Rubrics Way	$39	
	1039-J	Multiple Intelligence Approaches to Assessment	$39	
	1045-J	Seven Pathways of Learning	$35	
	1086-J	Intelligence Builders for Every Student	$25	
	1705-J	MI In Action	$245	
	1811-J	Tap Your Multiple Intelligences	$27	
	1914-J	Step Beyond Your Limits	$175	

Subtotal		
Sales Tax (AZ residents, 5%)		
S & H (10% of subtotal, min. $4.00)		
Total (U.S.funds only)		

CANADA: add 22% for S & H and G.S.T.

Name _____

Address _____

City _____

State _____ Zip _____

Phone (_____) _____

email _____

Method of payment (check one):

❏ Check or Money Order ❏ Visa

❏ MasterCard ❏ Purchase Order Attached

Credit Card No. _____

Expires _____

Signature _____

☎ **ORDER TODAY!**

Please include your phone number in case we have questions about your order.

▶ **To order write or call:**

Zephyr Press ®

P.O. Box 66006-J
Tucson, AZ 85728-6006

(800) 232-2187
FAX (520) 323-9402
http://www.zephyrpress.com